THE THIRD WAY

LOUIS M. HOUSTON

Copyright © 2023 Louis M. Houston.

All rights reserved. No part of this book may be reproduced, stored, or transmitted by any means—whether auditory, graphic, mechanical, or electronic—without written permission of both publisher and author, except in the case of brief excerpts used in critical articles and reviews. Unauthorized reproduction of any part of this work is illegal and is punishable by law.

ISBN: 979-8-89031-800-8 (sc)
ISBN: 979-8-89031-801-5 (hc)
ISBN: 979-8-89031-802-2 (e)

Because of the dynamic nature of the Internet, any web addresses or links contained in this book may have changed since publication and may no longer be valid. The views expressed in this work are solely those of the author and do not necessarily reflect the views of the publisher, and the publisher hereby disclaims any responsibility for them.

One Galleria Blvd., Suite 1900, Metairie, LA 70001
(504) 702-6708

CONTENTS

Acknowledgements 1
Preface 3

Background 5
The problem 6
The solution 6
Synopsis 7
Physics 14
Psychology 32
Philosophy 42
Spirituality 51
Metaphysics 59
Abstract 60
Free Association 60
Reflections 74

About the Author 83

ACKNOWLEDGEMENTS

I am indebted to my friends and family for providing support and being a source of inspiration for many ideas. This book is a culmination of a learning process that began many years ago. I owe a lot to Buddhism because of its excellent concepts. However, physics is my fundamental source, as it is my field of study.

PREFACE

We spend most of our lives searching for some form of fulfillment. We want to understand our purpose in life and we want to know how to get the most out of life. Family, friends, education and experience can support our worldview, but often we fall short of our goals and our overall search for meaning. Science provides a great deal of knowledge about the universe, but the significant questions remain. To make matters worse, there is the element of violence and the significant presence of corruption in our societies that makes life even more challenging and in some cases, more dangerous. In order to get answers to the deeper questions, we seek refuge in religion, philosophy, and spirituality. The challenges created by our mortality, our emotional instabilities and our intellectual obstacles make our lives even more difficult. We really want to know what it all means and how to navigate our way through it. Based primarily on a combination of physics and psychology, the third way proposes a method for training the mind to improve its thinking and stability and to derive a non-dual state of being that offers a perspective on every major discipline and that maintains an overall positive tone.

A metaphorm is a system that has characteristics that relate to each other the way characteristics relate in a different system. For example, pressure is a metaphorm for voltage since pressure stimulates the flow of fluid while voltage stimulates the flow of electrical charge. In this book, charged masses are a metaphorm for thoughts, as thoughts will be described as localized objects that interact in the way that charged masses do. The energy of thought will be treated in the same way as the energy of a charged mass. This allows us to use basic physics to describe the interactions of thoughts. Throughout this book, we will refer to physical quantities as they pertain to psychological functions.

We are interested in effecting a consistent network of thought patterns that conserve kinetic and potential energy as high-grade energy. Thought patterns with high-grade energy are maximally organized. Organized thinking is consistent with intelligence, while disorganized thinking can cause confusion, mood swings and irrational behavior.

There are three systems to consider: the physical system, the emotional system, and the intellectual system. The first way is to control the physical system. The second way is to control the emotional system. The third way is to control the intellectual system.

BACKGROUND

A human being is born with a variable response to the environment. We will refer to the environment as the universe. In order to survive and to successfully manipulate elements of the universe, a human being must learn how to behave. The behavior of a human being must be consistent with the constraints imposed by genetics, societal laws, and universal laws. When this is not the case, there will be conflict and disorganization resulting in the decline of functionality. In order to maximize degrees of freedom in behavior, a human being must find a way to minimize the effects of constraints. Ideally, the actions of a human being should have maximal variation while maintaining maximal consistency with the universe. The principle is simple. We can't eradicate the constraints, but if we reduce the size of the constraints, there will be more space to move around them. From the perspective of a human being, the universe is a network of concepts. If we compress the concepts, they occupy less mental space. As a result, there is more mental freedom. It is important that our compressed concepts remain valid and true. If that is not the case, then we become subject to destructive interference effects between our actions and the actions of the universe.

When our thoughts and subsequently our actions are consistent with the universe, we maintain a high grade of energy. High-grade energy is highly organized while low-grade energy is highly disorganized. An example of high-grade energy is electricity and an example of low-grade energy is heat. We can show that all of the major systems of thought have as their goal the acquisition of high-grade energy. These systems range from religion to science to philosophy and to spirituality. They all have the same goal, although that goal is expressed in different ways. Religions promote the elimination of conflict. That requires organized behavior. Science seeks to understand the universe. That requires knowledge that is highly organized. Philosophy seeks the truth. The truth is pure and untainted. Spirituality wants to connect to the essence of the universe. That requires the greatest subtlety.

THE PROBLEM

Inconsistent thoughts collide and either attach or damage one another. This is an inelastic collision that disorganizes the thought energy. Besides degradation of the energy, inelastic collisions can cause blockages and destructive scattering of thought patterns. This can result in personality changes, depression, and irrational behavior.

THE SOLUTION

The solution seems to consist of two stages. The first stage is to remove the mental blockages by allowing extreme thought patterns to interact. Eventually, only the cooperative thought patterns containing potential energy remain coupled to one another. The residual thought patterns are like plasma with their own separate charges. At this point, there is a lot of mental energy. The second stage of the solution is to selectively combine thought patterns so that neutral clusters are created. The desired cluster is binary. These clusters are highly abstract and are therefore highly compressed. The result is a network of largely neutral clusters of sparse thought patterns. These sparse clusters have minimal velocities because of the law of abstraction.

That is, the product of abstraction and velocity is a constant for a thought pattern. Therefore, the higher the abstraction, the lower the velocity and the lower the abstraction, the higher the velocity. The low velocities of the sparse clusters decrease the probability of inelastic collisions and therefore promote high-grade energy and consistent thinking. The balance of kinetic energy and negative potential energy results in zero total energy. Out of this equilibrium state emerges a positivity referred to a meta-positivity that creates intellectual clarity.

SYNOPSIS

Meditation is the process of observation without interference. It is often used as a tool to relax with and to detach from thinking patterns. Typically, meditation requires that an individual sits still in a lotus position and focuses on their breathing. Sometimes chanting is involved. Essentially, meditation includes simple repetitious activity. The meditation that we propose is to develop a completely open mind about events and concepts. What was previously off limits will now be considered. The good and the bad will be observed equally. This will initially cause consternation and unrest as conflict ensues. Abide by this conflict until things settle down. Eventually, the more cooperative concepts will dominate. Originally, this meditation was referred to as meta-duality, the name referring to the proposal to move beyond extremes by observing as extremes interact freely. Eventually, unstable attachments will become disrupted and concepts will become isolated. This creates plasma of highly active, but highly disorganized mental energy.

At this point, concepts can be specifically organized. We propose that these isolated concepts are combined into interactive clusters that are stable and that contain negative potential energy. In other words, these clusters contain high-grade energy.

When you specifically organize your thoughts, you are using concentration. Concentration is the complimentary process to meditation. The most compressed conceptual cluster is a binary cluster. That is, the cluster consists of two complimentary concepts. A binary cluster is compressed in the sense that examination of the cluster reveals implicit information. When we examine the cluster to reveal the implicit information, we are essentially unpacking the cluster. Unpacking is a form of decompression.

For example, the cluster meditation/concentration can be unpacked to reveal one process that intentionally does not interfere with thoughts while the thoughts interact to produce their natural disposition and to reveal another process that intentionally interferes with thoughts to produce an artificial disposition. The cluster points to another cluster: non-interference/interference and since interference can be constructive or destructive, it follows that concentration can yield either a positive or a negative result. This unpacked information points to another cluster: decondition/condition. Meditation deconditions the mind/ brain while concentration conditions the mind/brain. While the deconditioning process requires patience and tolerance, the conditioning process requires skill and precision.

The aforementioned paragraph represents some of the information that is implicitly contained within meditation/concentration. Rather than fill our mind/brain with that information, we only retain the original binary cluster. When we examine the cluster, we unpack it. This is the conditioning process that replaces the clutter in the mind/ brain with sparse, compressed thought patterns.

An isolated concept can be thought of as being charged in the sense that it radiates a force field that either attracts or repels other concepts. When that isolated concept is no longer isolated, but combined with a complimentary concept of equal strength, then the cluster becomes shielded from other concepts so that a minimal force is imparted. It is in this way that specific clusters are primarily neutral and when the mind/brain is dominated by neutral clusters, there is very little internal conflict.

We refer to the process of producing neutral conceptual clusters as meta-conditioning.

One might imagine that it would be beneficial to fill the mind/brain with isolated, positive concepts. This would create positive charge and desirable consequences. The problem with that approach is the nature of dualism. It is the nature of reality that meaning is derived from dual relationships. Therefore, in order for meaning to exist, dual concepts must exist. This implies that if we attempt to fill our mind/brain with good, then evil will manifest in order to maintain meaning. It is best to create the cluster, good/ evil that is neutral. This can be shown in a different way by proving that there is no essential difference between opposites and compliments. The evidence derives from the cluster, negative one/positive one. It can be easily transformed into zero/one by adding one and dividing by two. This proves that if one isolated charge exists, then its opposite must exist, since they are also complimentary.

Meta-conditioning is the process which neutralizes the mind/brain. However, within that neutrality there is an intrinsic positive energy. This is very much like the positive energy within the vacuum called the zero-point energy. An alternative way to think about it is through the proposition that everything is empty. Even emptiness is empty. Thus, emptiness is full. This brings to mind the cluster, emptiness/ fullness.

The kinetic energy of moving thought patterns is counter-balanced by the negative potential energy of neutral clusters. This negative potential energy is much like gravitational energy. The stronger the gravity, the greater is the negative potential energy. Similarly, the stronger the cluster, the greater is the negative potential energy. Therefore, meta-conditioning is enhanced by the production of powerful clusters.

There are several conclusions that can be drawn from emptiness/ fullness. First, as we have already mentioned, if even emptiness is full, then complete emptiness contains positive energy such as the zero-point energy of the vacuum. Secondly, we find that something can be derived from nothing or that pure creativity is possible. This leads us to the conclusion that death is not final or that within death there is a continuation of life. This conclusion is consistent with a conservation of spiritual energy. It is also consistent with a continuous emptying and re-filling of reality. That is, the universe exists as an endless succession of creation and collapse. The concept that when emptiness is empty, it is full suggests that there is no fundamental polarity or that positive can be equated to negative. This follows from the fact that the negative of a negative is positive and that if everything is negative, including negative, then negative is also positive. Another result of emptiness/fullness is the fact that even the inert contains energy. If we equate the inert to mass, we find that mass equals energy. This is, of course the neutral cluster mass/energy and the equivalence of mass to energy follows from the special theory of relativity. The importance of mass/energy is the fact that it is generated by emptiness/fullness, so we can see that emptiness/fullness is more fundamental than mass/energy.

Therefore, when we unpack emptiness/fullness, one of the elements is mass/energy.

Consider the cluster whole/part. A whole consists of parts. From one perspective, no one part can be identified with the whole. In this sense, the whole is empty. From another perspective, every part can be identified with the whole. In this sense, the whole is full. Thus, whole/part generates emptiness/fullness. The parts of a whole are extended indefinitely in exchange and interaction. Therefore, every whole is a part of every other whole. We can therefore say that every whole is a part, but not every part is a whole. By definition, the universe is the largest whole. Nonetheless, the universe is a part of every other whole. This is a holographic principle that points to the infinite self-similarity of reality. The whole/part cluster demonstrates that there is no such thing as a completely isolated system. An example of this is that even a black hole cannot indefinitely capture a particle. Therefore, even a black hole is not completely isolated.

It is clear that there are many neutral clusters. Therefore it is important that there exists a hierarchy of clusters such that unpacking a higher cluster produces lower clusters. In that sense, there is no need to maintain more than the highest cluster. We propose that whole/part is the highest neutral cluster. Whole/part generates emptiness/fullness that generates mass/energy and positive/negative. At this point, we can introduce the cluster action/reaction that is generated by positive/negative. We know that Newton's third law of physics states that to each action there is an equal and opposite reaction. Action/reaction generates push/pull that generates the three forces of nature, gravity/ strong/ electro-weak. Since the three forces of nature account for all physical phenomena in the universe, we argue that whole/ part completely describes the universe, both physically and spiritually.

We might question how whole/part can generate seemingly unrelated clusters like meditation/ concentration. Whole/part generates emptiness/ fullness. Emptiness/fullness generates mass/energy. Mass/energy generates particle/wave. Particle/ wave generates non-interference/ interference. Non-interference/ interference generates meditation/concentration.

As another example of unpacking, consider how whole/part can generate mind/brain. Whole/part generates emptiness/ fullness. Emptiness/ fullness generates mass/energy. Mass/ energy generates hardware/software. Hardware/software generates brain/mind or mind/brain. When we unpack this way, by moving from one neutral cluster to another neutral cluster, we maintain neutrality.

We have described how the vacuum contains a net positive energy. Thus, in pure emptiness, there is positivity. We refer to this as meta-positivity. Meta-positivity is the positive energy contained in neutrality. When there is a balance of polarity, there is only neutrality, but within neutrality there is meta-positivity. The goal of meta-conditioning is to fill the mind/brain with high-grade energy that is ultimately neutral, being a balance of positive kinetic energy and negative potential energy. When that balance is achieved and there is perfect neutrality, the mind/ brain will become meta-positive, just like the universe.

There will be a residual field created by isolated concepts that are not contained in the neutral clusters produced by meta-conditioning. Since we want this field to be zero, we must continue to meditate by keeping an open mind/brain that accepts extremes with complete tolerance.

Our thinking reflects the activities we observe and participate in. When we observe and participate in activities containing conflict and which cause damage to ourselves and/or to others, we promote disorganized thinking and low-grade energy. Whether our intentions are good or bad, it is not to anyone's benefit to sustain disorganized thinking. Therefore, the desire to be motivated by high-grade energy is non-dual, going beyond good and evil. It is essentially the desire to maximize intelligent behavior. Meta-positivity is non-dual because it exists only after a perfect balance of positive and negative is achieved.

When an individual obtains a state of meta-positivity, that individual will be beyond excitement or extreme emotion. Excitement or extreme emotion occurs when concepts accelerate towards or away from one another. When neutral clusters are present, concepts will execute minimal motion because the elements of a cluster are self-interacting and minimize any residual force field.

The size of a concept is its field of influence. Therefore the size of a neutral cluster is minimal. As pointed out earlier, our goal is to compress concepts so that they are effectively smaller. When we reduce the field of influence or the force field, we make the concepts smaller. This allows us to minimize the effect of constraints on our behavior and increase the space within our consciousness.

We point out that there is a significant difference between attraction that is due to negative potential energy and attachments that are due to deformations. Deformations occur with inelastic collisions in which the kinetic energy is not conserved. In certain deformations, concepts stick to each other while in other deformations concepts disassemble or decompose.

If we intentionally perform an action that causes conflict and damage, then we must have conceptualized the conflict and damage prior to the action. When we conceptualize conflict and damage, we degrade the energy of our thought patterns. This can cause confusion, mood swings, and irrational behavior.

Newton's third law states that every action has an equal and opposite reaction. If you inflict good upon someone, that good will be inflicted upon you. If you inflict bad upon someone, that bad will be inflicted upon you. Clearly, the damaging action that you cause others is not only a cause of degradation to your mental energy, but it will return to you. Of course, the same type of two-fold effect occurs for actions that promote harmony and organization. That is, when we act in a way that promotes harmony and organization, that action will return to us and will reinforce the harmonious and organized thought patterns that initiated the original action. So, while it is beneficial to organize our thoughts, it is even more beneficial to extend that organization into the outer universe.

Recall that the law of abstraction states that the product of abstraction and velocity is a constant for a thought pattern. We can interpret this law in terms of physics if we identify the abstraction of a thought pattern with its mass. In that case the law of abstraction becomes conservation of momentum. That is, in a closed system, the product of mass and velocity is a constant. Therefore, the more abstract a thought pattern is, the more mass it carries. This is consistent with the fact that the more abstract a thought pattern is, the more implicit information it represents. We point out that even in inelastic collisions there is conservation of momentum. Therefore, the law of abstraction will hold for all cases, unless there is an external force involved.

It is important to discuss a significant neutral cluster. That is, the Chinese pair known as the yin and the yang (i.e., yin/ yang). The yin and the yang are the complimentary forces that define the dark and bright elements of dualism in the universe. Every person has a mixture of yin and yang natures. The yin is implicit, dark and patient. The yang is explicit, bright and impetuous. The yin absorbs while the yang transmits. The yin is philosophical, intuitive and passive, while the yang is mathematical, logical and active. The yin and yang natures are a product of the Tao, the fundamental driving force of the universe.

PHYSICS

Most of human effort is directed towards living a rewarding life and different people go about this in different ways. There are disciplines such as religion and philosophy that aim to direct us towards the best life, but their approaches are varied and sundry. Consequently, it is difficult to select the best approach to living a good life.

We find the solution to the problem of living the best life by combining the wisdom from different belief systems and knowledge from science.

Energy produced by conflict and damage is low-grade energy. Energy produced by harmony is high-grade energy. Thoughts produced by conflict and damage are low-grade thoughts. Thoughts produced by harmony are high-grade thoughts. Energy flows from the physical system to the emotional system. It continues to flow from the emotional system to the intellectual system. The energy tends to be degraded as it flows from system to system. Although it seems unlikely, it is certainly true that our thoughts are influenced by the food we consume.

The fundamental goal in life is to maximize high-grade energy flow. We are sustained by the flow of energy through the yin and yang channels. When the yin energy is blocked, it becomes implosive. When the yang energy is blocked, it becomes explosive. There is the problem of imbalance that increases the energy flow through a single channel and there is the problem of energy degradation that is due to intrinsic resistance in a system. The increased energy flow can "burn" out a system through resistive heating. The problem is that the rate at which the energy is consumed is greater than the rate at which the energy flows. This is the problem with many illnesses. The problem is an imbalance in energy. As presented earlier, there are three major systems in the body: the physical system, the emotional system, and the intellectual system.

The energy flows from one system to the next. It can become degraded within any system as it flows. Energy can originate in an imbalanced state and it can also have any level of degradation. The problem with the consumption of meat is the energy is highly degraded because it has been processed by a higher life form. Vegetarians consume higher-grade energy because plants do not process energy to a large degree. Energy consumed from violent acts is degraded by the resistivity of the action. Energy consumed from harmonious acts is high grade because there is minimal resistivity. This does not require that we balance our yin and yang channels, but balanced channels reduce the probability that the energy will be significantly degraded because it reduces the rate at which we must consume energy within a single channel. In order to reduce the resistivity of a system, we must remove conflicting components. We must induce harmony within a system. In order to increase energy balance, we must develop both of our yin and yang natures.

It is well known that attachment leads to suffering. The problem is that attachment causes thoughts to cling to one another that, in turn degrades energy because it represents inelastic collisions. Meditation lubricates thoughts so that they do not cling to one another. This reduces energy degradation. When energy is degraded in the physical system, it can cause illness. When energy is degraded in the emotional system, it can cause mood-swings. When energy is degraded in the intellectual system, it can cause irrationality.

You should not force your thoughts to be a certain way. You should open your thinking up to all possible thoughts. That will necessarily include both good and bad thoughts, but eventually what we think of as good thoughts will prevail. If I restrict myself to having only good thoughts, then my thoughts will lose their meaning because there is no contrast. If I restrict myself to having only bad thoughts then my thoughts will lose their meaning because there is no contrast. A good thought is a coherent signal. A bad thought is an incoherent signal. Good thoughts will grow as N, while bad thoughts will grow as the square root of N. So the concept is to open your mind to all types of thoughts and wait until good thoughts dominate. This is meta-duality. When we restrict our thoughts to either good or bad, we eventually lose intrinsic meaning. As a result, we are subject to arbitrary dictates of morality and arbitrary meaning. When we open ourselves to both good and bad thoughts, there is an intrinsic, consistent meaning. As a consequence, there is an intrinsic, consistent morality. With meta-duality there is no need for rules and regulations because there is no need to impose meaning. It follows that by employing meta-duality, we enable ourselves to discover the true meaning of reality. The challenge with meta-duality is to not act on our thoughts until coherent thinking dominates our mind. This is a form of meditation. We open our mind to all thoughts and then we ignore them until coherent thoughts emerge.

It seems that by following preconceived notions of behavior, we inadvertently induce incoherency because the mind is so complex. The principle is that coherent thoughts grow as N, while incoherent thoughts grow as the square root of N. Coherent thoughts attract more coherent thoughts, while incoherent thoughts attract more incoherent thoughts. A mind/brain that is open to all thoughts will eventually become coherent. In contrast, if we limit the mind/brain, we can inadvertently induce incoherency because we select the wrong function. Is that function universal or does it vary from individual to individual? Due to variation in personality and intelligence, that function must vary from individual to individual. This is another reason why standard rules of thinking (i.e., behavior) are not appropriate for every individual. Furthermore, if our minds are closed systems, then incoherency will grow. In addition, the universe is dynamic, so the mind must also be dynamic. Rules of thinking are fixed and may partially be effective for finite periods, but they may become ineffective as the universe changes. Meta-duality is a dynamic process.

Meta-duality is about deriving a coherent and dynamic mental functioning. The key is that there are no rules. Rules are a problem in deriving coherency, because of the tremendous complexity of the mind/brain and its interactions with the universe. When rules are flawed, they can inadvertently induce incoherency. The challenge is to learn to ignore thoughts with meditation, so that unstable combinations of thoughts do not lead to action.

A rule is a barrier. The more rules we follow, the more barriers we create. When our mind/brain is filled with barriers, it becomes a closed system, unless the rules are carefully crafted. Based on the second law of thermodynamics, in a closed system, incoherency will grow. Consequently, we must keep ourselves open by having a minimal number of rules or by carefully constructing our rules. Mathematics is an example of a system with a large number of carefully constructed rules.

With meta-duality we adopt a system that has minimal selectivity. The growth of coherency is based on the random walk model. Given an equal number of coherent and incoherent thoughts, the rate of convergence of meta-duality is the square root of N, where N is the total number of coherent thoughts. Consequently, with meta-duality, progress is not linear. It's a time-consuming process. If we have nine coherent thoughts and nine incoherent thoughts, the ratio of coherency to incoherency will eventually become three.

The law of abstraction is as follows. The product of thought velocity and thought abstraction is a constant. If you want to decrease thought velocity, then increase thought abstraction. If you want to increase thought velocity, then decrease thought abstraction. You increase thought abstraction by encoding concepts into their fundamental components and by removing the extraneous details. For example, consider the neutral cluster, emptiness/fullness. (We will use the terminology "set" and "cluster" interchangeably.) According to the law of abstraction, thought velocity is minimal when abstraction is maximal. Emptiness has maximal abstraction because everything is fundamentally empty. The problem is that emptiness is singular. Consequently, it is highly interactive and can produce strong attachment.

The solution is to combine emptiness with fullness, its dual component. Emptiness/fullness becomes neutral. Singular concepts are interactive and can lead to either repulsion or attachment. The solution is to combine singular concepts with their companion concepts. This can become binary or tertiary or a larger set. A sparse set is abstract and thus correlates to slow moving thoughts. It is also neutral because it is internally interactive. Consequently, a sparse set is smooth. In order to increase thought velocity, we must reduce abstraction. That implies the inclusion of conceptual details. However, in order to avoid attachment, we must incorporate complete sets. A complete set is one that is internally interactive. An incomplete set is one that externally interactive. The members of a sparse set must be complimentary and categorically related. We can easily construct sparse sets. For example, energy becomes energy/mass and information becomes information/symbol. In each set, one element is the tangible representation of the other. It is clear that thinking in terms of sparse sets becomes slower and more fluid. It becomes slower because there is more abstraction and it becomes more fluid because the sets are neutral. The purpose of a sparse set is to increase fluidity.

Neutrality is a feature of emptiness. When we recognize that neutrality is equilibrium, we see that neutrality is essentially equivalent to emptiness. Just as meta-positivity emerges from emptiness, it also emerges from neutrality or equilibrium. Applying physics to the mind/brain, we find that thoughts experience velocity, force, and energy. We have already discussed the state of zero energy that occurs when the kinetic energy of thought patterns counter the negative potential energy of neutral clusters. The zero-energy state is a still point in the mind/brain just as the vacuum is a still point in the physical universe. There are two more still points. That is, the zero-force state occurs when the forces in the mind/brain are in equilibrium. In this state, thought patterns are not accelerating. Since desire accelerates thought patterns, it follows that in the zero-force state, desire is minimal. A third still point in the mind/brain is the zero-velocity state in which thought patterns are in stasis.

One might imagine that the zero-velocity state can occur during intense meditation when the mind/brain focuses on a single object.

While the still points created by zero-force and zero-velocity have been recognized by ancient spiritual traditions, the still-point created by zero-energy with the combined process of meta-duality and meta-conditioning is a new discovery.

Since each still point represents equilibrium, we find that meta-positivity can emerge in each case. With reference to the still point of zero-energy, we emphasize that the energy must be high grade. There must be minimal heat energy in the mind/brain if a still point is to be reached.

Normally, positive and negative energy in the mind/brain is a result of external forces. In contrast, meta-positivity is purely internal. It emanates from the structure of the mind/ brain itself. In other words our mood is ordinarily a result of our external influences. So, if we are in a good mood, it is because we have had a positive experience. Alternatively, if we are in a bad mood, it is because we have had a negative experience. With meta-positivity, we are given a good mood even while in isolation, because the source of our positivity is internal.

In the same way that we can relate psychological phenomena to physics, we find that we can interpret the yin and yang channels as the right and left hemispheric functions of the mind/brain, respectively. It is commonly known that the right side of the mind/brain is responsible for artistic and philosophical thought while the left side of the mind/brain is responsible for scientific and mathematical thought. It is clear to see that if we explore their relative functionalities, we find the right and left hemispheres comparable to the characteristics of the yin and the yang. Based on this relationship, it follows that since our experience and behavior is always a product of our mental/cerebral functionality, then our experience and behavior are always channeled through our yin and yang natures. The balance between our yin and yang natures is equivalent to the balance between our right and left hemispheric functions.

It is interesting to consider the contrasting constraints of the mind/brain when the different still points exist. We find that there is increasing variance. The still point of velocity allows no motion in the mind/brain. The still point of force allows motion but no acceleration. The still point of energy allows acceleration but no heat. There is stability to the still points. That is, the still point of velocity will exclude a field of motion. The still point of force will exclude a field of force and the still point of energy will exclude a field of heat. There is, of course, a limit to this field exclusion. If the fields are large enough, the stability will be broken. Obviously, the still point of velocity presents the largest constraint, while the still point of energy presents the smallest constraint. Consequently, reaching the still point of energy is the most reasonable goal if one is to compress constraint and allow more space and flexibility within the mind/brain.

We can observe the resonance between the still points and the various systems. The still point of velocity resonates with the physical system and one might imagine that it is easier to acquire stasis within the physical system than within the emotional or intellectual systems. The still point of force resonates with the emotional system since desire is a force and the suppression of desire is a well-known spiritual goal. The still point of energy resonates with the intellectual system since it excludes disorganized thought patterns or heat. We can designate the physical system as mass/energy. The emotional system can be designated as emotion/desire. The intellectual system is, of course, designated as mind/brain. Observe that the well-known dualism, mind/body is equivalent to mass/energy with mass being a metaphor for body and energy being a metaphor for mind.

Each still point generates a meta-positivity that manifests in the physical system as physical energy. It manifests in the emotional system as emotional energy and it manifests in the intellectual system as intellectual energy. Therefore, when meta-positivity gives us extra vitality, it is due to a still point in velocity. When meta-positivity gives us a good feeling, it is due to a still point in force. When meta-positivity gives us mental clarity, it is due to a still point in energy.

If we designate the mind/brain as the inner universe and the physical, societal environment as the outer universe, then our system is dual consisting of the inner and outer universes. When we reach the still point in energy which excludes heat from the inner universe, the exclusion force runs counter to thermodynamics, which requires that two interacting systems reach thermal equilibrium. That is, when the outer universe has more heat than the inner universe, there will be a tendency for heat to flow from the outer universe into the inner universe, until both systems are in thermal equilibrium. The exclusion principle prevents this equilibrium unless the difference between the systems becomes too great. The limit of the exclusion force places a limit on meta-positivity, maintaining it at a minimal level.

The exclusion principle designates the exclusion of heat from the zero-energy state within the inner universe. We can explicitly identify the exclusion principle. In physics, it is known as the principle of least action and in philosophy, it is known as Occam's razor. The principle of least action states that given multiple paths for the flow of energy, a system will choose the path of least action or the path upon which the energy-time is minimal. In philosophy, Occam's razor states that given multiple solutions to a problem, the simplest solution is the best. If we identify heat as the product of inconsistency or disorganization, it follows that the path of least action is the path that minimizes heat. Similarly, the solution that minimizes complexity will tend to be the solution that minimizes heat. Therefore, the consistency or organization of the inner universe will tend to reinforce it and cause it to remain stable, counter to the influences of the outer universe. The requirement is that the inner universe reaches the still point that includes a critical level of organization.

We can also identify the exclusion principles for the other two still points. The still point for velocity excludes velocity.

This is consistent with Newton's first law of physics which states that a body at rest will remain at rest until acted on by an external force and a body in motion will remain in motion until acted on by an external force. Essentially Newton's first law is the law of inertia. Inertia is a property of mass and therefore in this context, inertia is a property of a thought pattern. A thought pattern at rest will tend to remain at rest until acted on by an external force. The still point for force excludes force. This is consistent with a stable equilibrium that when displaced from equilibrium will experience a restoring force that moves it back towards equilibrium. An example of stable equilibrium is a spring. When applied to a thought pattern in stable equilibrium, we find that if the pattern is accelerated, it will decelerate towards its equilibrium state.

We can propose a meditation that activates all three still points, simultaneously. That is, we focus on the cluster whole/part. Since whole/part is the highest neutral cluster, it unpacks into all other significant neutral clusters. Remaining focused solely on whole/part until whole merges into part as a single concept implies zero velocity and thus the zero-velocity still point. Since whole/part and all associated clusters are neutral, there is a minimal residual force field produced. This causes the zero-force still point. Finally, the negative potential energy contained in whole/ part is counter-balanced by the kinetic energy contained in the motion from the constituent concepts, whole and part. Consequently, the total energy vanishes and the energy still point is reached. In point of fact, with continued meditation, as the concepts whole and part merge, there is stasis with zero potential energy, again resulting in the zero-energy still point.

It was previously proposed that the largest whole was the universe. A different argument might be presented from a more spiritual perspective. That is, the largest whole is infinite and thus, whole/part becomes infinite/finite. This can be interpreted as being equivalent to the cluster God/ man, (man is representative of both male and female) so that the largest whole is equivalent to God. Therefore, whole/part incorporates the highest spiritual component. God would have to exist outside of time, since the universe is being created and destroyed continuously throughout time. This follows from the continual emptying of emptiness, in which emptiness is the fundamental state of the universe.

With respect to God/man, it is clear that man is a part of God, but since every whole is a part, then God is a part of man.

A list of selected neutral clusters are whole/part, emptiness/ fullness, God/man, infinite/finite, physical/emotional/ intellectual, reality/ universe, positive/negative, mass/energy, mind/brain, particle/ wave, one/zero, yin/yang, action/reaction, software/hardware, non-interference/interference, logic/ intuition, push/pull, gravity/strong/ electroweak, meditation/ concentration, imaginary/real, and emotion/ desire. All of these clusters are generated from the fundamental cluster, whole/part.

If we generate concepts that violate these clusters, we produce disorganized energy or heat within the mind/brain. The fact that all of these clusters are compressed into whole/ part demonstrates the size reduction of the constraints these clusters represent. Whole/part contains maximal abstraction and therefore minimal velocity. Because its velocity is minimal, it is less likely to have a collision with another thought pattern. In and of itself, whole/part has no controversial meaning on a moral, political, or societal level. Therefore, it doesn't come into conflict with any other concepts. However, it contains the fundamental conceptual elements of reality. Despite the neutrality of whole/part due to the symmetry of its components, there remains a sense of asymmetry due to the apparent superior nature of whole as compared to part. This gives one a sense of the meta-positivity that emerges from its intrinsic neutrality.

In a stable system, the heat in the outer universe remains less than the energy of exclusion required to maintain meta-positivity in the inner universe. However, heat from the outer universe can overwhelm our inner universe and overcome our exclusion energy or make it difficult for us to reach a still point. Meditation and meta-conditioning can help immensely, but our ultimate success at excluding heat depends on our particular life circumstance. If we happen to live in an extremely disorganized environment, we must seek refuge in places with more harmony. At that point, we can continue our efforts to reach meta-positivity.

In order to reach the still point of velocity, we must learn to control our physical system. In order to reach the still point of force, we must learn to control our emotional system. In order to reach the still point of energy, we must learn to control our intellectual system. Controlling physical systems is the way of technology and martial arts. Controlling emotional systems is the way of psychology and spirituality. Controlling intellectual systems is the way of logic and philosophy. We refer to the particular way to control the intellect discussed in this book as the third way.

A way, in this context, is a way to reach a higher state of being. In today's society, technology and science is the predominant way. It is a way of physical systems. In the ancient world, martial arts were the more common physical way.

The way of spirituality seeks to suppress inordinate desire and emotion. This is generally achieved through some form of meditation. The higher state of being reached through spirituality is called enlightenment.

The third way seeks to suppress disorganized thinking. This is achieved through meditation and mental programming. The higher state of being reached through the third way is called meta-positivity. The third way frames all three higher states of being as forms of meta-positivity.

The third way uses physics to model mental processes. This is not done in a traditional way that includes cerebral processing. Rather, we model abstraction as mass and treat the motion of a thought pattern as we treat the motion of a mass. This relationship is a consistent metaphor in which the thought pattern is a metaphorm for a charged mass.

Unlike the other ways, the third way is consistent with both science and spirituality. We might express this as a neutral cluster, science/spirituality. It is important in the third way to have a consistent paradigm for thinking about all elements of reality, because inconsistency produces heat energy.

Given a still point, many concepts in the mind/brain will remain isolated and thus charged. A charged concept will cause a force field. Nonetheless, the force field does not have to produce heat because the motion of thought patterns could remain organized.

During the process of meta-conditioning, neutral conceptual clusters are created. In the interest of brevity, refer to the fundamental neutral cluster as the primary. When we unpack or decompress the primary into its constituent clusters, we expand the space of consciousness around the primary. After we compress the clusters back into the primary, we leave a vacant region of expanded space. Application of adiabatic cooling, that stipulates that pressure decreases as volume expands dictates that the temperature decreases with the increased volume. Since temperature is proportional to heat, it follows that adiabatic decompression and isothermal compression about the primary reduces the heat content. In addition, when we immerse ourselves in a harmonious environment, which is essentially cool, the heat in our system will diffuse into that environment and our system will cool down.

In the third way, we seek a balance between negative and positive energy and the exclusion of heat. Therefore, energy must be in equilibrium and it must be organized before meta-positivity emerges. Meta-positivity is the product of cool neutrality. The concept that positivity can be a property of neutrality is non-dual and it is consistent with the positive energy residual produced by the vacuum state of the outer universe. This positive energy residual is responsible for the acceleration of the expansion of the universe. When meta-positivity is sustained in the mind/brain, it causes consciousness to incrementally expand, resulting in further cooling.

We might imagine that it is desirable for the mind/brain not to be in equilibrium, but to have a surplus of negative or positive energy. However, if that is the case, because of the nature of dualism, the imbalance will eventually cause a loss of meaning. Negative energy is yin and positive energy is yang. Yin is not necessarily bad and yang is not necessarily good, but when something is bad, it is also yin and when something is good, it is also yang. We can conclude from this that there is no sustainable environment in which everything is either perfectly good or perfectly bad. The universe must contain both good and bad in order for it to be sustainable.

Awareness of a cluster is positive energy, while the cluster itself contains negative energy. There is equilibrium between the awareness of a cluster and its nature. When we unpack or decompress a cluster, we can generate more clusters and/ or individual concepts. The individual concepts will produce a force field that accelerates thought patterns. This will increase the kinetic energy and represents a conversion from the potential energy of the original cluster. At this point, the energy is not in equilibrium because there is a surplus of kinetic energy. Equilibrium is regained when the concepts are compressed into the original cluster. The compression also simultaneously cools down the consciousness. (Note that when we refer to consciousness, we are also referring to the space of awareness within the mind/brain.)

Essentially, the goal of the third way is to keep cool. That is, we want to avoid heating the mind/brain. A cool mind/ brain is highly organized while a hot mind/brain is highly disorganized. In the physical universe, heat is a natural quantity and it is often desirable. In fact, human beings are warm-blooded. Nonetheless, we want to avoid disorganized thinking that can result in conflict and damage, physically, emotionally, and/or intellectually.

Recall that the exclusion principle is the tendency to exclude velocity, force, or heat in order to maintain a still point that includes meta-positivity. When we tend to exclude heat, we will naturally avoid situations that incorporate disorganized concepts. This may manifest as an apparent lack of interest, but it is actually an aversion to inconsistency. The exclusion principle, in this case, is a mechanism that keeps the inner universe cool. Our personality will be affected by the exclusion principle, as it will influence our likes and dislikes. It is important to remember that the exclusion principle is an element of the mental programming incorporated into the third way. When we begin to experience the exclusion principle, we will acquire evidence that the programming is effective.

When we practice the meditation known as meta-duality, we open ourselves up to extremes, letting diverse and sundry concepts interact freely within our mind/brain. This meditation will decompose improper clusters and allow proper clusters to form. An improper cluster is one that is not neutral, but maintains a field of influence. Stress/anxiety is an example of an improper cluster, since it radiates a field of repulsion, although the component concepts interact strongly. Fear/anger is another example of an improper cluster. Meditation will decompose these clusters and the component concepts can be dissipated into a cooler environment.

When we refer to a cluster as being neutral, we are applying an approximation, because there is a residual field, which leaks from the cluster. If there was not a residual field, we would not be able to examine the cluster and decompress it. So we can imagine that a cluster produces a residual force, but no heat. Continued exposure to the cluster will cause it to reach complete equilibrium, such that there is no residual force and the cluster is thoroughly neutral. At this point, there is zero energy and zero force. Eventually, with further exposure to the cluster, the component concepts will merge into a single concept and there will be no conceptual motion upon examination. At this point, there is zero energy, zero force, and zero velocity. This describes the simultaneous acquisition of the three still points. We might well imagine that the cluster will eventually absorb itself and vanish, but mass/energy is conserved. Therefore, there are no other still points.

The heat capacity of a material is a measure of the material's ability to absorb heat without significant changes in temperature. Since temperature is a measure of disorganized energy, in terms of the mind/brain, the heat capacity is a measure of its tolerance to heat without becoming significantly disorganized. The heat capacity varies with materials and it is a natural property. We propose that the conceptual heat capacity is a measure of the intelligence of the mind/brain. Therefore, intelligence is a natural characteristic of the mind/brain and it is intrinsic to the structure of the mind/brain. In this context, intelligence is the ability to tolerate heat. While it is clear that intelligence is an advantage for someone following the third way, high intelligence is not a prerequisite. In order to be successful, one simply has to adhere to the method.

Consciousness is the space of awareness within our mind/ brain or inner universe. It can be focused on the contents of the inner universe itself or it can be focused on the contents of the outer universe. When we expand our consciousness, we expand our awareness and broaden our viewpoint. Consciousness is obfuscated by extreme experiences such as pain or pleasure and it is enhanced by neutrality. Therefore, when we reach a still point and our mind/brain is in equilibrium, our consciousness has maximal clarity. This allows us to make a more objective analysis of the universe.

We acknowledge the reference to concepts as charged masses. That suggests the influence of both electromagnetism and gravity. There are two other forces in the universe, the weak force and the strong force. Normally, the weak force is merged with electromagnetism into the electro-weak force. Electromagnetism is due to the interaction of charged particles, while gravity is due to the interaction of masses. The weak force is responsible for radioactive decay, while the strong force holds the nucleus of an atom together and acts only over short distances. We find a correlation to the weak force in the mind/brain with reference to an isolated concept. If kept in isolation, a concept will lose meaning. This decay of meaning correlates to the weak force. There is also a correlation to the strong force within the mind/brain. That is, the complimentary concepts within a cluster are subject to a strong force that compresses them into a single concept. In this sense, we see that all of the forces of nature are represented within the mind/brain.

The unification of electromagnetism with the weak force occurs at extremely high temperatures. In the context of the mind/brain, the weak force represents loss of meaning. Electromagnetism is charge interaction that, with respect to the contrast between concepts, can be interpreted as meaning. Essentially, meaning derives from the way concepts influence each other and that influence derives from the force field of the concept that derives from its charge. At high enough temperatures, charges have no influence. This represents loss of meaning that is decay. At this point, electromagnetism combines with the weak force.

The activity of the electro-weak force suggests an environment that consists of a soup of concepts that have undifferentiated meaning. The strong force, that is only active over short distances, is responsible for merging clusters of concepts into individual concepts. Since the strong force requires minimal separation, it will only activate at even higher temperatures than those required for the electro-weak force.

Gravity requires mass or in this context, abstraction. At the initial point of expansion of the universe, there is maximal abstraction. This suggests that the order of emergence of the forces into existence within the inner universe is gravity, the strong force, the weak force, and electromagnetism.

Meaning is the motive force for the flow of information. Therefore, meaning is intrinsic to the energy of a thought pattern. Meaning is vibrational in the sense that it expands and contracts in continuous cycles. The universe is created and contracts with the cycle of the expansion and contraction of meaning. When the universe is completely empty, meaning is completely contracted. When the universe is empty of emptiness or full, meaning is completely expanded. Human beings are currently living in a period of the expansion of the universe, both physically and in terms of meaning.

Abstraction is equivalent to mass. It is a measure of the density of information within a concept. The density of information is equal to the information per length. The primary, whole/part is the most abstract concept that can be understood. It is interesting that according to the third way, a singularity has infinite abstraction and zero meaning. This is consistent with the fact that within a black hole, the laws of physics break down.

The exclusion of heat from the inner universe implies the exclusion of entropy or disorder. According to the second law of thermodynamics, the entropy in a closed system will never decrease. However, if the system is open and connected to another system, transferring heat into the second system can decrease entropy within the first system. This is a property of the relationship between the inner universe and the outer universe. That is, heat and entropy within the inner universe is reduced at the expense of an increase of heat and entropy within the outer universe. When energy is entropic or disordered, it is difficult for the energy to do work. Some speculate that the universe is gradually becoming more entropic and will decay until there is no possibility to extract work from it. An alternative concept, consistent with what we show in this book, is that the universe will expand and eventually collapse in endless cycles. Therefore, entropy will maximize and minimize as the universe cycles. One obvious conclusion is that entropy cycles with meaning. At the beginning of this phase of the universe, there was zero entropy and zero meaning. In short, there is always a balance of meaning and entropy in the universe.

Since a thought pattern is charged, its velocity is proportional to an electrical current. When an electrical current passes through a path of resistance, it produces a phenomenon known as Joule heating. Essentially, in Joule heating, the local environment of the current radiates heat. If there is no resistance there is no heat and without resistance, the current persists without decay. In this case, the current is in a superconducting state. Consequently, the exclusion of heat by the mind/brain creates a superconducting state and the temperature of the mind/brain remains at or below a critical temperature. The superconducting state is consistent with a state of minimal entropy. An external magnetic field can reduce the superconductivity, but we find there is an exclusion principle known as the Meissner effect. The Meissner effect repels a magnetic field from a superconductor, unless the magnetic field is above a critical level. We find that the Meissner effect is equivalent to the exclusion principle for heat included in the third way.

There is another interesting relationship between superconductivity and the third way. Normally, electrical current is comprised of individual electrons. In this context, we can relate an electron to an isolated concept. In superconductivity, the electrons are in binary clusters called Cooper pairs. The pairing of electrons into Cooper pairs is seen as the significant cause of the superconducting state. It is interesting to compare Cooper pairs to the neutral conceptual clusters of the third way.

In short, the third way is a method for producing a superconducting mental state.

PSYCHOLOGY

We might ask ourselves, what constitutes a higher state of being and how do we get there? It would seem that acquiring a higher state of being means becoming a better person. This could mean becoming stronger, smarter, wiser, friendlier, more loving or any number of decidedly good things. So it seems that there are many characteristics that we could change or improve in order to reach a higher state of being. Based on the third way, there is only one characteristic that we need to improve in order to reach a higher state of being: consistency. That is, we aim to reduce disorganized thinking. When we think consistently, we maximize the effectiveness of our intelligence. If our intelligence is maximally effective, we make better decisions and improve our life.

The goal of the third way is zero net energy and the exclusion of heat. We can interpret negative energy as the motivation behind inward exploration of the inner universe. Positive energy is the motivation behind outward exploration of the outer universe. When the inward and outward motivations are balanced, there is zero energy. Some would refer to inward exploration as introspection and outward exploration as extrospection. Heat energy is highly disorganized and does not produce much work. When there is heat in our thinking, it results in disorganized thought patterns that are not useful in making effective decisions. Disorganized thinking results in disorganized actions. Therefore, in addition to acquiring zero energy in our thinking, we need to exclude heat.

When there is zero energy and minimal heat in our thinking, we reach what has been referred to as a still point. A still point is a point of equilibrium or balance. When a still point is maintained, it becomes a reservoir of creativity and it can produce a subtle positive energy referred to a meta-positivity. Meta-positivity is similar to having exhausted our reserves of physical energy and suddenly acquiring an adrenaline rush. It is like writing a beautiful story after being in deep depression. It is like finding the perfect solution after being stumped by a problem for a long time. The only difference is that meta-positivity is subtle and takes us only slightly above equilibrium. Meta-positivity is so subtle because is does not deplete the contrast between extremes as would happen if we were saturated with positive energy. Without a significant contrast between extremes, in this case, positive and negative energy, our thinking would lose meaning.

There are two other still points, one for zero velocity and another for zero force. Zero velocity or stasis focuses on physical systems, such as the human body. We reach a still point when we are able to remain perfectly still. Zero force suggests a lack of violence and/or a lack of desire. The still point associated with zero force exists in the emotions.

It follows that meta-positivity for each still point comes in different forms. For zero velocity, it is a physical boost. For zero force, it is an emotional boost and for zero energy, it is an intellectual boost.

Dualism is the contrast of opposites or compliments such as black and white or man and woman. We acquire meaning from dualism. However, meta-positivity is non-dual because it is not derived from the selection of positive over negative. Rather, it derives from the balance between positive and negative.

Reaching the third still point is the goal of the third way. However, the third way includes the methods needed to acquire the other two still points. Meditation on a single concept can lead to all three still points. In this book, we demonstrate a binary combination that is referred to as the primary concept. Upon examination, the primary concept generates all other significant concepts. If we meditate on this primary concept, we can eventually reach all three still points. The primary concept is whole/part.

The third way aims to improve the intellect, but includes the methods to improve the body and the emotions. A person who improves any one of these systems moves into a higher state of being. Meta-positivity is the positive overtone that accompanies this higher state.

We point out that every action begins in the imagination. Therefore, conceptual consistency leads to harmonious actions. Every major component of systems that have sought the improvement of the human condition is consistent with the third way. These components include love, compassion, non-violence, and passive resistance.

Most of our mental activity exists in the space called the unconscious. The unconscious is the region where thoughts are hidden from awareness. However, every conscious thought pattern eventually resides in the unconscious, so that activities that require meditation eventually take complete mental effect. Therefore, we must be patient when practicing the third way. All good things come in time.

It is important to understand what is meant by consistent mental activity. Consistent, is this case does not refer to disorganized behavior and it does not refer to activity that destructively opposes other activity. This may be confusing because one might interpret chaotic activity as being consistent because it is thoroughly chaotic or seems to exhibit similar confused patterns. Consistent mental activity, in this context, refers to smooth mental activity that does not possess any contradictory behavior that causes conflict and damage. We would not consider the behavior of a child to be consistent because of the spurious, contradictory behavior that a child typically exhibits. We would not consider the behavior of a calm, sociopath to be consistent, because a sociopath kills people, causing severe destruction. We define consistent behavior as behavior that is compatible to itself at both small and large scales. Using this concise but precise definition of consistent, we are able to designate a particular mental state that is indifferent to good or evil, but that resonates with positivity.

The third way does not consist of a list of spiritual rules or laws such as the Ten Commandments or the eight-fold path. It does not have a morality and it is not spiritual. It is simply an exploitation of physics projected into the psychological domain. Essentially, the third way promotes the exclusion of heat. In the physical sense, heat refers to disorganized energy. Therefore, in the psychological sense, heat can also be interpreted as disorganized mental energy. The third way has a prerequisite. That is, we must probe the inner universe as much as we probe the outer universe. This causes equilibrium in our total mental energy. We might interpret this equilibrium as a balance between our yin and yang natures.

There are two stages to the third way. The first stage requires meditation and the second stage requires concentration. We use meditation to decondition ourselves from inconsistent notions by opening our thinking to consider various and sundry opposites and compliments. Inconsistencies that have become bad habits will decompose because of their exposure to extreme ideas that were never before considered. In time, we will learn the more consistent and cooperative combinations of ideas. However, our thoughts may be highly active at this point, because of the high level of interactivity between the remaining ideas. This will cause a certain level of confusion. Concentration, the compliment of meditation, now comes into play. We concentrate in order to organize our thoughts so that complimentary ideas are combined into what has been referred to as conceptual clusters. These clusters are minimal when they consist of two complimentary concepts or when they are binary. When properly organized, we find that these clusters simplify information into a form of compression or encoding so that by studying or examining a cluster, we can expand it into the representative information it contains. These clusters can account for a lot of ideas and by using them, we remove a lot of mental clutter. The sort of mental examination associated with the expansion of a cluster is the result of energy that is positive because it counters the negative potential energy of the cluster. Therefore, the creation of conceptual clusters promotes a balance between positive and negative mental energy.

The completion of the second stage of the third way may leave a residual quantity of disorganized mental energy that is small relative to the overall mental stability. This disorganized mental energy or heat is reduced by the action of compression and decompression of ideas and by exposing ourselves to harmonious environments. Soothing music, hot baths, interesting conversations, good books, beautiful scenery and solitude are all examples of harmonious quantities.

Earlier in the book, we referred to the mental environment as the mind/brain. This terminology is a binary cluster that represents the complimentary components of our thinking. Such clusters are readily used in descriptions within this book. The primary conceptual cluster was defined as whole/ part. We call this the primary cluster because by examining it, we can derive all of the other significant conceptual clusters. This hierarchy and containment allows us to use whole/part as the focus of the meditation that derives the three still points. Whole/part might be compared to the Hindu sound, Om, which represents the beginning, duration, and dissolution of the universe.

The third way is a form of mental programming because it rearranges mental concepts by using language. It has been said that we are what we eat. It is also true that we are what we think. By changing our thinking, we can change our lives. While the substance of the outer universe is mass/energy, the substance of the inner universe is abstraction/meaning. From the perspective of mental programming, these substances are the same. Meaning or the flow of information in the mind/ brain is energy in the reality/universe and abstraction in the mind/brain is mass in the reality/universe. Because we are naturally programmed by genetics, society and our physical environment, efforts like the third way must be intense and precise in order to counter our other influences. While the third way promotes consistency, it is its own consistency as software that determines its integrity and stability.

The problem is that life places constraints on our behavior. In order to minimize the constraints, we must minimize the way we conceive of them. Traditionally, there are barriers that separate the different aspects of our life. Those barriers add complexity to the systems we deal with. This added complexity means that there are separate theories for every discipline. Complexity enhances the probability of inconsistencies. The language of the third way incorporates all of the significant ideas of physics, psychology, philosophy, and spirituality into one system. As a consequence, there is less complexity and fewer opportunities for inconsistencies. The unification of these disciplines in the third way allows it to produce concise and efficient software and gives it the ability to handle life's constraints in a universal way.

The stability of the mental programming provided by the third way culminates into a restoring force that heals the software if it is damaged. This might be referred to as a regenerative ability. The result of this restoring force is a field of influence produced by the inner universe. That is, the outer universe will experience a certain level of order and harmony at the boundary between universes. In common language, we are referring to the situation when a person is giving off positive vibes.

The mental conditioning used by the third way is called meta-conditioning because it aims to take the mind/ brain into a positive state that emerges from the balance between positive and negative. That positive state is called meta-positivity. This is a non-dual concept, because in dualism, there is only neutrality when positive is balanced with negative. Meta-positivity might be described as a peaceful state.

We must understand that we are essentially a collection of ideas. How well we survive and hopefully thrive is dependent on how those ideas interact with each other and with the environment. The third way is a small set of ideas that when absorbed promotes our ability to thrive. It is maximally compatible with all other ideas because it is based on physics, a well-tested and well-supported science.

We might think of the mind as the software and the brain as the hardware of our intellectual system. While both components are essential, only one, the mind has significant flexibility to enable us to control our behavior. Therefore, we focus on the mind and the mental programming we impose is a function of the mind. Since the mind can only be programmed to optimize its joint interaction with the brain, our behavior is limited by what particular brain we genetically inherit. This represents another fundamental constraint in our lives.

The main attribute that we want to mentally program is consistency, both in thought and in action, but this can be difficult to discern. Many would classify violence as consistent because it is uniformly chaotic. However, violence, by definition, is not compatible with itself. In fact, uniformly violent behavior is often mistaken for consistent behavior and it is for that reason that it can become attractive to some. We are also, at times, drawn to violence because it seems to be the easier path. Think about the energy A, required to create something and then think about the energy B, required to destroy it. It would seem that A>B, but energy is conserved, so A=B. However, the grade of the energy must be reduced by the destruction. The destructive energy has more entropy or disorder than the creative energy. Since entropy has a tendency to increase, we are naturally drawn to behavior that increases entropy.

Consistent behavior is causal. Causality is the property of nature that links cause to effect into a form of meaningful continuity. In order to envision causality, think of a serial arrangement of boxes. When one box falls, it causes the neighboring box to fall. This can cause a cascade of falling boxes. Imagine how we might interpret the situation if the last box fell before the third box fell. In that case there would be no causality and the falling boxes would lose meaning. In short, without causality, there is no meaning and without meaning, there is no flow of information.

Causality brings to mind that there must be an order to our ideas. That is idea (1) is followed by idea (2) that is followed by idea (3) and so forth. Consequently, we cannot just immerse our hardware in an ensemble of ideas. The ideas must have structure. Furthermore, it is clear that either causality or the disruption of causality leads us to the source of our behavior. There is a reason for everything. That reason has more clarity if a system has more causality within its structure. Therefore, if our mental programming is well structured, we are better able to trouble-shoot our system when errors are encountered. In other words, implementation of methods like the third way empowers self-examination so that corrections can be made efficiently. This is certainly a benefit because it is not uncommon to be confused about our behavior and how to rectify it.

Given a sequence of thought patterns, the chain of causality may be tightly linked or weakly linked. That is, the variation in the relationship between sequential thought patterns may be low or it may be high. Yet, in either case, a causal connection is maintained. The ability to select thought patterns with varying levels of causality is typically designated as free will. Clearly, if we select thought patterns with no relationship whatsoever, we move into the realm of irrational thinking and there is zero causality.

If there is a specific determination in the relationship between sequential thought patterns or between sequential physical events, then the causality is deterministic and prescribed by physical laws. In that case, causality is tightly linked. However, if the causality is weakly linked, physical laws may not determine the relationship between sequential events, but the relationship retains a harmony or compatibility that is not inconsistent with physical laws and discernible upon careful examination. As an example of the comparison between determinism and causality, consider the first case of a bowling ball striking a pin. The effect of the pin falling is a deterministic fact based on the law of conservation of momentum. In the second case, consider the action of eating a meal after washing your hands. There is no deterministic relationship, but it is causally meaningful that one washes hands before having a meal and the sequence of events does not violate any physical law. This explains the difference between determinism and causality. Clearly, we want our inner universe to be causal, but not deterministic, since we want to maximize our freedom but retain adherence to the constraints imposed by physical laws.

Given the fact that an effect diminishes with distance, we must emphasize the personal perspective as the primary perspective. However, when we consider ideologies, we must incorporate connectivity, because there is no such thing as perfect isolation. That is, isolation is an approximation because everything is connected. We have already stipulated that every whole is a part of every other whole because the parts of a whole are indefinitely extended through interaction and exchange. Consider the fact that the air molecules we breathe have been processed by countless other individuals. The importance of connectivity in the third way diminishes the role of ego. A diminished ego is consistent with psychological health and enhanced spirituality.

We need to resolve the meanings of opposites attract and like attracts like. They are opposing concepts, but each seems to be valid. This is simply explained. Opposites attract when there is a deficit of meaning. When there is a surplus of meaning, like attracts like. In the mental environment produced by the third way, there is a surplus of meaning because there is equilibrium between dual states. Therefore, a personality influenced by the third way will attract similarly organized systems.

Emotions are the result of attractive and repulsive forces on concepts. In the third way, mental programming combines complimentary concepts into clusters so that attraction and repulsion is largely neutralized outside the perimeter of a cluster. As a result, emotions are retained but become marginal, unless concentration decompresses a conceptual cluster and discloses individual concepts. Since the individual concepts are charged, they are subject to acceleration and can cause intense emotional expression.

A real significant point is that the third way enhances intelligence. While intelligence is mostly inherited, acquiring mental flexibility and clarity of thought can enhance it. Intelligence is the ability to manipulate information. Information flow is functionally equivalent to mental energy. The higher the grade of energy, the more readily it can be transformed into different forms. Because the third way promotes the incorporation of high-grade mental energy, the individual is better able to manipulate that energy. Consequently, that individual will possess an enhanced intelligence.

Thinking that is conditioned by the third way is also more logically consistent. Because the conceptual clusters produced by meta-conditioning are largely neutral, there is minimal interference, and therefore logical processing is smooth and has continuity. The third way enhances the imagination and the ability to communicate. When the mind/brain has less clutter because concepts are compressed and there is an abundance of mental space, there is room for speculation and theoretical modeling. In addition, the approximate neutrality of the resident conceptual clusters creates a compatibility with the imagination. Imaginative thinking makes the mind/brain more flexible and open to various and sundry scenarios. Therefore, communication with other individuals is more readily performed. Essentially, the third way makes the mind/brain more open to different possibilities that do not conflict with the laws of physics and the correlative laws of psychology and philosophy.

The rate of motion or velocity of thought can be controlled by the compression and decompression of conceptual clusters. Recall that the law of abstraction states that the level of abstraction of a thought pattern times its velocity is a constant. Therefore, a compressed neutral cluster moves slowly while a decompressed cluster that consists of conceptual details moves fast. There is more meaning for faster motion and this is consistent with the fact that meaning is the motive force behind the flow of information.

PHILOSOPHY

Consider the topics, order, free will, morality, existence, essence, reality and imagination, knowledge, truth, power, reason, nihilism, being and nothingness as they relate to the third way.

Order implies consistent behavior and organization. That is, order represents behavior that is compatible to itself at all scales. The third way promotes order. It is an order that is consistent with equilibrium or balance. Since there is always disorder in the outer universe, order in the inner universe will retain meaning based on its contrast with the outer universe. The opposite of order, disorder is equivalent to entropy, a quantity that increases as the universe expands. Order suggests an underlying structure, while pure disorder is structure-less. Based on the third way, order is the most important quantity. Order is an attribute of high-grade energy, while disorder is an attribute of low-grade energy. The challenge is to segregate order and disorder despite the inclination of disorder to invade order. We propose that life, itself is the segregation of order and disorder, so that the third way is consistent with the persistence of life. The ordering of energy into a zero sum is indicative of inward probing of the inner universe balanced with the outward exploration of the outer universe. There is a natural complimentary ordering of abstraction and meaning. We find that the greater the abstraction, the less the meaning and vice versa. Order is a component of every system, whether that system is music, science, mathematics, or art. Information requires order. Therefore, there would be no communication without order. While order is intrinsic to the macroscopic universe, disorder is intrinsic to the microscopic universe.

Free will is the motive behind behavior that is not strictly deterministic. Strict determinism occurs when prior events are the direct cause of a current event and the cause produces the effect by the transfer of energy. Free will allows for a weaker connection between cause and effect such that there are many possible effects. The third way enables a sparse mental environment with considerable space. Therefore, there is room for significant variation in thought patterns. This makes a perfect environment for the enactment of free will. Unless a sequence of thought patterns becomes chaotic, free will is still causal. In other words, free will maintains a cause and effect relationship. This is indicative of rational behavior. There is some debate as to the validity of free will given the nature of macroscopic physics that allows one to predict the outcome of events given the initial conditions. Consider the following argument for the existence of free will. Given a transition from point A to point B, the principle of least action states that nature will select the most efficient path between the points. For example, when lightning strikes, it finds the most efficient path to ground or when a boulder rolls down a mountain, it takes the most direct route. After an event has happened in which our action or sequence of actions have taken us from some point A to some point B, we are typically able to examine the path taken and construct improvements that will include some alternate path. In other words, we are typically able to imagine a better path between A and B. However, that particular path was not taken. If we had no real choice or free will and were simply an agent of nature and determinism, the principle of least action would have taken us through the most efficient path. Therefore, in hindsight, we never would imagine a better path because the best path was already taken. In short, free will must exist because, after a path is taken, we can typically imagine a better path.

Morality is the sense of right and wrong. The third way advocates non-violent actions because violence is indicative of low-grade energy. In society, it is generally recognized that non-violence is right and violence is wrong. Therefore, it follows that the third way is consistent with morality. In the interest of deconditioning the mind/brain from false or improper concepts, the meditative stage of the third way is open to different possibilities, including what might be considered wrong actions. However, ultimately, what is wrong is that which is disorganized and the more organized activities eventually dominate the content of our thoughts. What is crucial to the meditative stage is the ability to ignore and mentally conceal wrong thoughts as they undergo dynamic interactions with right thoughts. We do not want to act on our thoughts until some measure of coherence is reached. This allows us to avoid immoral actions while simultaneously meditating on both moral and immoral thoughts. The second stage of the third way involves the incorporation of complimentary concepts that represent physical principles. These principles project themselves into the psychological arena metaphorically and maintain consistent meaning. From this perspective, morality is derived from the extrapolation of physical principles into non-physical systems. The acquisition of high-grade energy, a major goal of the third way, is consistent with a high moral standard, but is independent of societal rules, the typical source of morality.

Existence is that which is as opposed to that which is not. It is that which comes into being or manifests. Existence is one side of the complimentary pair, manifestation/potential. When something has potential it will manifest and when it no longer manifests, it becomes potential. The universe is continuously coming into and out of existence as it cycles through expansion and collapse. We are continuously coming into and out of existence as we cycle through birth and death. The third way relies on a fundamental principle. That is, emptiness is the fundamental state of the universe. Everything is empty, even emptiness. Pure emptiness is potential, but not existence. Empty emptiness is manifestation or existence. The emptying of emptiness is the process that brings everything into and out of existence. How can we know whether or not we exist? Existence implies both meaning and suffering. Suffering is the consequence of low-grade energy or more explicitly, entropy. Meaning expands as entropy expands with manifestation. If we know meaning and/or if we suffer, we exist. Alternatively, existence is a result of the asymmetry between the waking world and dreams. That is, we can tell the difference between a dream and existence. There are some who believe that existence is an illusion and that what we experience is simply a product of the mind/brain. If that were the case, then we would never suffer, because the universe would be constructed to satisfy our every need. However, everyone suffers at some point in their life and that is evidence that life is not an illusion.

Essence is the core ingredient. It is the internal source of being. Essence is the platform upon which everything is constructed. From a mental programming perspective, the fundamental essence of the third way is the primary conceptual cluster, whole/part. Spiritually, we might interpret whole as infinite or God. An essence is empty in the sense that it has minimal meaning. It is full in the sense that it has maximal abstraction. Based on the law of abstraction, a concept with maximal abstraction has minimal velocity. Therefore, an essence undergoes minimal change. The fact that our essence is largely infinite is equivalent to it being largely in finite. That is, the essence is within the core of the finite and it is essentially infinite. This is indicative of the holographic principle that implies that global structure is locally contained. Thousands of years ago, it was surmised that the essence of matter was the atom. An atom is primarily composed of space and is therefore mostly empty, consistent with the notions of the third way. An atom is both a whole and a part, since it contains elementary particles, but is a part of a structure known as a molecule. From the perspective of the third way, the essential concept is a generator of lower order concepts. In that sense, the ordering of what is typically considered to be an essence is inverted. That is, in the third way the essence is the concept that expands into all other significant concepts. Consequently, the essence is the key mental ingredient, existing at the highest level. In contrast, an essence might be thought of as the most common ingredient, such as an atom, that is at the lower limit of hierarchy in the structure of matter.

Reality is that which exists or has existed. It is substantially equivalent to existence, but it incorporates existence in a historical sense. For example, I exist, but Abraham Lincoln does not exist. However, I am real and Abraham Lincoln is real. We normally contrast something that is real with something that is a fake or an imitation. Therefore, being real suggests that something is substantial or tangible. However, something that is real may itself be intangible while having a significant effect on certain tangible things. An example is Newton's third law: to each action there is an equal and opposite reaction. This example essentially points to the reality of a particular concept. Reality has roles in two different binary clusters. Reality is the subtler component of reality/universe, that is similar to mind/brain, and it is the more substantial component of reality/imagination. Reality is in contrast to imagination that is not a part of existence, but that exists in a different space. Reality is constrained by logical and physical laws. However, imagination has no constraint. Therefore, while some imaginary items have the potential to exist, the incompatibility of other imaginary items with logical and physical laws precludes them from existence. Therefore, the space of imagination is larger than the space of reality. Reality is something that is either physical or has an impact on the physical world. Elements of the imagination that have no pertinence to the physical world are considered to be abstract and therefore, lacking in meaning. In fact, the act of manifestation is largely equivalent to bringing something from being abstract into being something that is concrete or real. In the sense that the third way incorporates both abstraction and meaning, it therefore includes imagination and reality. This is consistent with the non-dual nature of the third way.

Knowledge is the information that forms the basis of understanding. When we have knowledge of something, we have the ability to enhance or disrupt its functionality. That is why knowledge is power. When we have knowledge of something, we also have the ability to interpret its functionality and communicate it to others. Therefore, knowledge is a necessary component of education. Knowledge also imparts the ability to analyze and reconstruct systems. Science donates to knowledge in a significant way. That is, a scientist forms a hypothesis about a system and then tests that hypothesis with an experiment. When a hypothesis develops coherency and rigor, it becomes a workable theory. The third way is primarily based on theoretical knowledge. However, that knowledge is supported by logical consistency and its coherence with other systems of thought. The fact that knowledge is information acquired over time and power is energy per unit time is consistent with the earlier statement that knowledge is power, since, information flow in the inner universe is congruent to energy in the outer universe and power, according to physics, is the rate of change of energy. Knowledge can be destructive. Physics determined that mass can be converted into energy and that led to the development of the atomic bomb and its obvious destructive capability. However, knowledge is predominately creative, since it enables one to derive meaning from abstract systems. It is important to note that when we refer to the extension of abstraction into what has meaning, what is meant is that abstraction becomes expanded or decompressed into meaning, since abstraction is defined as information density. In the sense that abstraction is expanded into meaning, this process is representative of the transformation of abstraction into meaning and to that extent, indicates an essential equivalence. Consequently, knowledge is the motive that transforms abstraction into meaning.

Truth is that which does not change. In that sense, it is substantially equivalent to essence. However, while essence is internal, truth can be either internal or external. When truth is internal, it is a local quantity. When truth is external, it is a global quantity. In the sense that truth does not change, it is consistent. Since consistency is essential to the third way, it aligns itself with the truth. The primary whole/part is proposed as truth, in the sense that it is the fundamental component of reality. Anything that works to give a system its functionality is the truth. Therefore, truth is functionality. Since truth is consistent, what is false is inconsistent. Therefore, something that is false contains contradictory behavior, such as heat energy. The psychological exclusion of heat is a goal of the third way. That is, the third way aims to exclude that which is false. It follows that all of the major disciplines seek to know the truth and that describes their major commonality. It is interesting to note that most things change, while the truth remains in stasis. Therefore, despite its major significance, the truth is a small fraction of reality. The truth generally comes in the form of compressed language, such as a set of equations or a poem or a single word. Truth is not inconsistent with imagination, since although it is not real, imagination may contain truthful concepts. Therefore, truth is inspirational and spurs growth and development. In its abstraction within the mind/brain, the truth creates the space for variation and diversity. That is, truth is compatible with freedom.

In physics, power is the rate of change of energy. Generally speaking, power is the ability to control. Consistent and effective functionality will naturally enhance power. Therefore, although power is not its only goal, the third way enhances power. Power can be exploited to do wrongful things, containing conflict and damage. However, power is also used for good, such as useful technological advancements and physical and mental conditioning, similar to what is proposed in the third way. Political power is the most widely known version of power, since it can have influence at the global level. The ability to control societies is a use of power that insinuates itself into diverse systems, including war, religion, government and communication networks. Natural physical systems can have tremendous power, such as the weather, the sun, and black holes. From that perspective, power controls the universe. Since power is the ability to change the flow of energy, it can allow for the redistribution of psychological energy, the essential action of meta-conditioning. It is clear that the exclusion principle for heat, responsible for mental stability in the third way, is a system of power since it alters the rate of change of heat energy within the inner universe with respect to the outer universe. There is a power struggle at the center of the third way, since it aims to decondition the individual from the negative influences of genetics, the environment, and society. The success of the third way is reflected in its ability to overpower previous influences.

Reason is the ability to study, analyze, and construct logical arguments. A reasonable argument or experience is causal. That is, there is a cause and effect relationship between sequential events. From that perspective, reason might be interpreted either as a causal system's sensitivity to causality or as the level of causality within a system.

Reasoning requires concentration and therefore, reasoning enables someone a level of control over his or her thoughts. Consequently, reasoning is the primary tool of the third way. Since concentration gives one the ability to expand meaning, reasoning is consistent with meaning. Reason is complimentary to intellect and thus, is part of the binary cluster, reason/intellect. When one has the ability to reason, one has the ability to categorize and organize, which counters the existence of heat. Reasoning allows one to design complex systems and is therefore the motive behind technological advancement. Reason/intellect is the hallmark of the human being and creates a separation from the inanimate, plants and animals. We point out that the cluster reason/intellect is generated by mind/brain. Therefore, reason/intellect is an attribute of mind/brain. Reasoning creates an objective perspective of reality and is more consistent with our yang nature. In contrast, emotions create a subjective perspective of reality and are more consistent with our yin nature. Reasoning enhances communication since communication propagates meaning. Reason is the motive force behind introspection and extrospection. Therefore, reason facilitates the balance between negative and positive mental energy.

In the theory proposed by the third way, the universe expands and contracts in endless cycles throughout time. Along with the universe, meaning also expands and contracts. Therefore, the conception of meaning proposed here is one of cyclic variation. In other words, meaning is not considered to be a constant quantity. This variation in meaning can occur with intent as a concept is compressed into minimal meaning or decompressed into maximal meaning. Clearly, in order for the theory of the third way to remain viable, there must always be a meta-meaning, even when meaning, itself has subsided. Without a meta-meaning, there can be no such theories as the third way, capable of describing periods in the universe when meaning is absent and periods when meaning is maximal. This discussion was a prelude to the concept of nihilism. Nihilism is a philosophy that sees an absence of meaning in the universe. Nihilism promotes chaos and destruction and runs counter to organization and harmony. Essentially, there is no meta-meaning in nihilism. There is no way or method to reach a higher state of being, because nihilism does not acknowledge the existence of a higher state of being. It is for this reason that people with nihilistic tendencies are often depressed. There is no hope or positivity in nihilism. The universe is seen as a place with no order or meaningful structure. There are elements of nihilism in the philosophy of existentialism and nihilism can be an erroneous result of interpreting the fundamental state of emptiness. Nihilism does not witness the balance in the universe between such quantities as the yin and the yang. Rather than dualism, nihilism sees only one state within the universe, the total absence of value and meaning.

Being is substantially equivalent to existence. However, there is the added quantity of consciousness. That is, a being has consciousness of the universe. In this sense, we attribute being to the state of a living thing. Therefore, there is no being in a rock and very little being in a plant. However, both an animal and a human have being. If we consider the level of consciousness to be proportional to the level of being, then a human has more being than an animal. Being may be a measure of value for the living and therefore, being creates hierarchical relationships. By increasing our attentiveness and level of perception, we increase our consciousness, and therefore our being. The third way requires an awareness of our inner functionality and the functionality of our environment. Therefore, the effectiveness of the third way depends on our level of being. Being develops as we mature. That is, an adult has more being than a baby. However, we may lose being as we get older and our mentality decays. If we go through life doing things with very little awareness, we diminish our being and also our ability to anticipate our experiences. Clearly, a being is a part of reality and is not a part of imagination. That is, a being is real. For the spiritual, God is the maximal being and to the extent that God is a part of us, God is our being. In terms of the third way, our being and thus, consciousness is infinite and in finite.

Nothingness is emptiness, the zero state. In terms of the evolution of the universe, nothingness is a period that has the potential to come into existence. Nothingness is a phase and not permanent, since the universe expands and contracts continuously. As emptiness, nothingness is the fundamental state of the universe. That is, everything is empty, even emptiness. There is a balance between emptiness and fullness and therefore, emptiness/fullness is an essential conceptual cluster. When we see emptiness as openness, space and potential, we understand its positive attributes. Of course, the fact that emptiness is the cause of fullness, its complimentary state, is its most positive attribute. Often emptiness or nothingness is interpreted as being solely negative and an element of nihilism. Thus, psychologically, emptiness can cause depression and lead to suicidal thoughts. This unfortunate misinterpretation can be avoided by careful analysis of emptiness. Neutrality is a form of emptiness in that it is empty of charge.

Equilibrium is a form of emptiness because there is a balance of extremes. In the third way, we seek neutrality and equilibrium in order to achieve a still point. Therefore, a still point is a point of emptiness. However, just as the emptiness of emptiness is fullness, a still point is a source of energy we term meta-positivity. The vacuum state of space contains positive energy due to the uncertainty principle of quantum mechanics. We refer to this still point energy as meta-positivity. Meta-positivity means that in complete emptiness, there emerges positive energy and this is the ultimate goal of the third way.

SPIRITUALITY

Consider the following spiritual topics: the soul, faith, sin, attachment, karma, reincarnation, God, heaven and hell, creation, and love and hate as they relate to the third way.

The soul is the non-physical essence that pervades the body through life and exits the body at death. The soul is the core identity of a person. Although it may acquire excess baggage, it is generally considered to remain pure and untainted throughout the course of one's life. Based on Eastern religion, the soul migrates from one lifetime to the next, although Buddhists do not believe in the soul. Christians believe that the soul moves from life to either heaven or hell. It has been said that the eyes are the windows to the soul, a figurative statement that proposes that the essence of a person is available through direct communication. The soul is often connected to the underlying truth so that it can be attributed to non-living systems and quantities. The existence of a soul has not been scientifically confirmed. That is the case for most, if not all spiritual matters. As with most spirituality, belief in the soul is primarily based on faith. Interpreted as the essence of being, the soul is maximally abstract and as abstraction, it does not change. This is consistent with the association of the soul with identity. It is commonly believed that an animal has no soul, however, there is some non-physical correlate that inhabits animals in order for continuity to exist between lifetimes. This unknown non-physical entity, not the soul, must also correlate to what is believed in Buddhism. The third way proposes a continuation of being across time that might be part of a meta-meaning. Perhaps this continuing being is the soul.

Faith might be thought of as belief without experimental evidence. However, faith is not purely theoretical, since there is no logic in faith. Faith is more closely related to intuition. It is the primary tool of religion, although many scientific discoveries have relied on faith. The neutral conceptual cluster logic/intuition is equivalent to logic/faith. Therefore, faith is complimentary to logic. In order to resolve abstraction, concentration is needed, but concentration is aided by faith. It follows that since God is the most abstract concept, faith facilitates belief in God. The primary cluster, whole/part is more easily resolved with faith and thus, the third way is enhanced by faith. Faith is not valid when it is inconsistent with logic. Unfortunately, many practice an invalid form of faith. For example, people of faith tend to believe that God created the universe at some time, approximately 13.7 billion years ago, during the Big Bang. However, more recent evidence is consistent with the theory that the universe endlessly expands and contracts over time and that the Big Bang was simply one expansion. Consequently, God would have to have created the reality/universe outside of time. Physicists believe that there are ten spatial dimensions and one time dimension. Seven of the spatial dimensions are undetectable because they are so small. Faith would have to be consistent with a God that exists outside of the eleven—dimensionality of space/time. The third way subscribes to faith in the sense of believing in a theory without experimental evidence. If the theory is logically consistent and robust, then it may have sufficient internal support without the need for experimental evidence and the theory may predict phenomena that are beyond the range of experimental evidence. In physics, string theory is a potential unified field theory or a theory of everything that is not supported by experimental evidence, but many have a lot of faith in it.

A sin is a wrongful action or state. Based on Western religion, as a wrongful action, a sin is a violation of any of the Ten Commandments. For example, one of the Commandments is thou shalt not kill. With respect to the third way, a sin is consistent with the deprivation and/or damage of functionality. Therefore, a sin, as a wrongful action, causes degradation in energy, in opposition to the primary goal of the third way. The difference between a sin, in the traditional sense, and that, which is avoided by the third way, is the specification of an assortment of rules. This specification is limiting and has the potential to lose congruence with a growing societal structure. A person can exist in a state of sin or in a wrongful state. This state correlates to having low-grade mental energy. Such a state may be caused by the presence of improper conceptual clusters such as fear/ anger. Recall that an improper cluster is not neutral despite interactivity and radiates a field of negative influence. The religious believe that God sent His only son, Jesus Christ to earth to be sacrificed in exchange for the original sins of mankind. This is suggestive that human beings intrinsically have low-grade energy or sinful tendencies. We live in a universe that contains a large quantity of heat and entropy, both physically and psychologically. The natural connectivity and exchange between different systems creates the propensity for the sharing of heat and entropy. Therefore, it is reasonable to find human beings struggling with the effects of disorder. The third way is a tool that aims to reduce psychological and consequentially, physical disorder.

An attachment is a clinging of the one to the other in such a way as to deform both the one and the other. Attachment is not to be confused with its precedent, attraction. In physics, two masses become attached after an inelastic collision in which kinetic energy is not conserved. The residual energy is transformed into lower grade heat energy. Consequently, the psychological interpretation of attachment is the effect of a collision between thought patterns that results in a merged, but deformed thought pattern accompanied by psychological disorganization. Buddhism sees attachment as the primary cause of suffering. This is consistent with the third way since attachment produces low-grade energy that can cause emotional and mental problems. This, in turn can lead to undesirable actions. The statement desire leads to suffering is suggestive that desire, as attraction can lead to attachment. Desire is a psychological force that accelerates thought patterns such that collisions are likely. Consequently, in order to avoid attachment, it is safer to minimize desire. The incorporation of neutral conceptual clusters minimizes force and therefore desire. This is part of the meta-conditioning stage of the third way. The component concepts of a cluster are attracted to one another in a way that minimizes any residual force. However, they do not deform one another and consequently, decompression can precisely expand a cluster into its implicit information.

Karma is the concept that an action is reciprocated by an equivalent action. As a consequence of karma, if we do good things, then we will experience good things and if we do bad things, then we will experience bad things. Therefore, karma is essentially a moral regulator. Newton's third law states that to every action, there is an equal and opposite reaction. We might interpret this in terms of karma. That is, actions that send energy away from us will result in reactions that return the same energy. Based on karma, every action has a consequence. The third way projects order and therefore it should cause one to experience an ordered response from the universe. Eastern religions propose that karma can cause activity over the span of different lifetimes, so that actions done in a previous life can cause reactions in the current life. This interpretation of karma enables an explanation for good and/or bad experiences that seem inexplicable, but are, in fact, reactions to behavior in a previous life. Karma is consistent with the golden rule, that is, do unto others, as you would have them do to you. Concepts like these are laws of reciprocity and point to a type of conservation of energy. It is clear that karma is a law or constraint that must be observed in order to experience success. The societal connectivity promoted by karma is consistent with the properties of whole/part in that every whole is a part of every other whole. Consequently, the integrity of one donates to the integrity of all.

Reincarnation is the continuity of being throughout different lifetimes. That is, we are born, we live, we die, and we are reborn to repeat the process. Reincarnation is consistent with the emptying of emptiness that sequentially produces emptiness and fullness in endless cycles. The universe continually expands and contracts and being lives and dies in a similar manner. Reincarnation has the energy of the cluster manifestation/potential. That is, reincarnation occurs as potential becomes manifestation and subsequently, manifestation becomes potential. Reincarnation is the migration of the soul and ceases only when the soul moves outside of time. Although Eastern religions believe in reincarnation, Western religions tend to believe in a single lifetime. Since reincarnation is consistent with the properties of emptiness and the universe, the third way incorporates reincarnation as a necessary element of spirituality. Many believe that a being can be reincarnated into different life forms, such as a plant or an animal. This depends on the grade of energy that one obtains in a given lifetime. If the grade of energy is consistently high enough, one may evolve to escape the wheel of life and move outside of time into the space of God. This existence is a state of maximal abstraction and minimal meaning. Therefore, it is a constant state that is consistent with truth and meta-meaning.

God is the single most important spiritual concept. However, the existence or non-existence of God has never been decisively proved. God is the creator of the reality/universe. Many question this because the universe seems to be in a continual cycle of existing and not existing, apparently without the need of a creator. The third way supports the existence of God as the most important concept, because God represents the infinite whole and whole/part is the primary neutral cluster. Simply put, the importance of God is clear since we either spend ample time trying to believe in Him or trying not to believe in Him. So, it is clear that whether or not God has a tangible existence is independent of His importance as a concept. If we accept the validity of God, then He must exist outside of normal space and time and the endless cycle of the universe must have been created outside of time. God is infinite and in finite. That is, every whole is a part of God and God is a part of every whole. The God concept has infinite abstraction and zero meaning. Based on the law of abstraction, God never changes and has infinite meta-meaning. It is difficult to see how God has zero meaning, but this implies that God is completely ordered and completely empty. Recall that emptiness is the fundamental state. The primary cluster, whole/part generates all of the significant clusters. Therefore, it is the only cluster that needs to be maintained in the mind/brain. The identification of whole/part with God suggests that God is the only necessary concept and that all other concepts derive from God. This implies that meditation on the God concept reveals the universe if we understand the properties of God.

Heaven is the harmonious afterlife in the space of God. We go to heaven after we live a life of minimal sin or after we live a good life. The concept of heaven is not typically consistent with reincarnation. However, reincarnation includes an evolution based on good behavior. A more consistent interpretation of heaven is that it exists outside of space and time after one has exited the wheel of life. In this sense, heaven is the repository of the enlightened. This particular interpretation is consistent with the third way if one acknowledges that there is a critically high-energy grade that excludes entropy such as the superconducting state. When the mind/brain acts as a superconductor, there is a constant state of being that no longer evolves. Being then resides in a state that is analogous to heaven. In heaven, one experiences meta-positivity as described by the third way. Clearly, the physical self will continue to experience entropy, despite meta-positivity. However, the psychological body will be free of degradation and in that sense, exist outside of space and time. Hell is the inharmonious afterlife that is the punishment for a sinful life. Hell is the opposite of heaven and it is a consistent de-evolution in the wheel of life. Believers in reincarnation do not believe in hell as an afterlife. However, they believe that if we live as a human in a wrongful way, we may reincarnate as a plant or an animal. Based on the third way, hell is a state of pure heat, in which no useful work can be extracted. If we allow ourselves to fall into a state of hell, there is no way to recover. Therefore, hell is a point of no return.

For many years, physics has claimed that the universe was created 13.7 billion years ago in a phenomenon called the Big Bang. Recent investigations suggest that the creation of the universe was one expansion in a ceaseless series of expansions and contractions. Therefore, the beginning of the universe was one beginning in an infinite number of beginnings. In every beginning of the universe, there is nothingness or emptiness. In that emptiness is the potential for creation and growth. In order to conceive of the creation of the reality/universe, we must imagine that it was created outside of time. In this context, any process must start and end outside of time. Our personal creation began outside of time and it must end outside of time. The third way will eventually move us outside of time in the process that finally creates us. Each way is capable of creation. The first way creates the perfect physical system. The second way creates the perfect emotional system. The third way creates the perfect intellectual system. The potential of each way exists within each of the three life forms, plant, animal, and human. The plant can reach a still point of velocity or stasis. The animal can reach a still point of force or zero desire. The human can reach a still point of energy with zero heat. In each still point is the emptiness that precedes creativity and from which emerges meta-positivity. We emphasize that a human has the capacity to reach all three still points and that the first and second ways have been practiced in different contexts by various spiritual traditions. The language of the third way includes each way and consolidates their total creative potential.

Love is the most harmonious emotion. Just as gravity is the essential force that unites the physical universe, love is the essential force that unites the psychological universe. Love is what inspires relationships and keeps families together. Love has spiritual value. It is the critical element of Christianity. In its truest form, it is unconditional. Love supports a higher state of being that opposes man's destructive tendencies. It has no specific structure, yet it is easily understood. As desire, love produces attraction without attachment. Love is compatible with all things. It includes empathy and compassion. However, love is purely emotional. Therefore, it has no intellectual content. It is clear that because love is an emotion, and emotional behavior predominates, then love continues to be the simplest tool for promoting societal harmony. In terms of the third way, love is a tool for reducing heat, since it avoids attachment. However, love is insufficient for manipulating the conceptual complexities of the universe. Hate is the opposite of love. As love is attractive, hate is repulsive. As love is subtle, hate is gross. Hate is consistent with heat and therefore, hate is precluded by the third way. The proliferation of hate in the psychological universe correlates with the growth of entropy in the physical universe. Based on dualism, love has no meaning without hate. However, the goal of the third way is to exclude hate from the inner universe. The balance of love and hate in the universe suggests that the eradication of hate will move us to a non-dual state in which love is unnecessary, but is replaced with meta-positivity.

METAPHYSICS

Reality is a set of interactive codes or software. Conceptual experiences manifest as representations. Therefore, the manipulation of concepts forms the basis for manipulating reality. Code must be written to supplement existing code that acts as a set of constraints. All experiences, systems and structure are the result of code. Attempts at domination by singular codes mandates defensive tactics. However, global sustainability is required for local integrity. Therefore, the best code is universally compatible. Experiential representations must be combined in code into a unified picture. This creates coding flexibility and can incorporate pre-existing coding constraints. Unification is enabled by mental consolidation based on structural metaphors. All disciplines have commonality as code. Therefore, computation is the only discipline. The universe is manifesting its most subtlest essence: code. This is evident in the proliferation of computing technology. Of course, computers are simply representations of concepts that form the basis of code. Programming is conditioning. Therefore, conditioning techniques based on the manipulation of language must be incorporated into programming. The third way is a code that unifies all other codes by using meditation and concentration in a complimentary manner. Meditation and concentration are representations that interact with the conceptual world to facilitate mental programming. The fundamental nature of computation means that there are actually no beliefs. There are only constraints. The objective of coding is to bypass constraints. However, smooth interpolation and extrapolation require a local compatibility with constraints. Obviously, if there were no constraints, coding would have no limits. However, constraints are a pre-existing condition of reality. An additional problem is that singular codes create more constraints because of their offensive strategies. Codes that produce conflict are in error because they are not sustainable. The details of reality reflect the complexity of its manifest code. It is a mistake to focus code on explicit representations. It is better to focus code on fundamental concepts. However, that which is termed fundamental remains mired in beliefs that are simply the epiphenomena of constraints. God is fundamental only because God represents code without constraints, not because God actually exists. Physics is fundamental because it accurately represents constraints. The venue used to present the third way appears at the level of belief, but that is an illusion created to smooth the impact of presentation. The third way is an attempt to make a code with minimal constraints.

ABSTRACT

The third way is an approach to mental conditioning that improves mood and thinking. The problem is that the mind is typically filled with various and sundry ideas. Because of a lack of compatibility, these ideas are compartmentalized and when they interact, there is often conflict and damage. The third way incorporates a language that allows these diverse ideas to be combined. Consequently, the mental environment simplifies and the mind has less clutter and more order and harmony.

FREE ASSOCIATION

Force is the ability to accelerate a mass. Emotion and concentration are both the ability to accelerate a thought. However, emotion is the unintentional acceleration of a thought and concentration is the intentional acceleration of a thought.

Manifestation transforms thoughts into reality. By using concentration, manifestation turns a concept into a representation. The sustained decompression of a conceptual cluster will lead to manifestation.

The uncertainty principle in quantum mechanics shows that knowledge is always incomplete because there are always residual uncertainties. Heat energy can cause random collisions that, in thoughts, can cause attachment and damage. The random collisions can be interpreted as mental uncertainties. The ground state or lowest energy state of a system retains energy because of the uncertainty principle. In the same way, the ground state of the mind/brain retains energy because of mental uncertainties.

In the sense that meaning is the motive behind the motion of a thought, meaning is proportional to pressure or voltage.

A peculiar fact is that the length of a thought sequence is proportional to its velocity and inversely proportional to its mass. However, the information content of a thought is proportional to its mass. In short, mass is information density. Therefore, the more complex a code is, the more mass it has. Since mass is equivalent to energy, complexity is equivalent to energy.

A belief is a constraint. If we minimize our beliefs, we minimize our constraints. Constraints are what separate reality from imagination. A constraint places a limit on our actions.

The primary code is whole/part. It generates all other significant codes.

The fundamental state is emptiness. It is encoded in emptiness/fullness. The emptying of emptiness is responsible for the endless cycle of potential and manifestation in the universe. It is also responsible for meta-positivity, the energy that emerges from a still point.

Abstraction is mass. Therefore, infinite abstraction is infinite mass. The equivalence of mass to energy implies that infinite abstraction is equivalent to infinite energy.

Similar to the effects of a black hole, a distortion of causality can be created by the presence of a concentrated mass within the mind. This provides an explanation for free will.

A lie is based on inconsistent thoughts that create collisions with the potential for attachment and damage. Therefore, a lie can hurt the source. A secret occurs when thoughts are isolated. This does not preclude internal consistency, so a secret does not degrade organization.

A mistake is an inconsistency. Therefore, the third way reduces mistakes.

Repetition of consistency increases consistency.

Repetition of inconsistency increases inconsistency.

The attraction to violence by the non-violent is a search for meaning because isolated concepts lose meaning.

Isolation is an approximate quantity because complete isolation does not exist.

Not only do we treat thoughts as masses, but we also give them charge to represent the influence of their conceptual content.

The conversion of abstraction into meaning is metaphorically equivalent to the conversion of mass into energy.

The third way is a metaphor that transforms physics into psychology.

Time moves slower when we are focused on abstraction and faster when we are focused on meaning.

Abstraction/meaning is a significant conceptual cluster that is metaphorically equivalent to mass/energy.

Meaning promotes motion. Abstraction promotes stasis.

It is not who we are that has meaning. It is what we do that has meaning.

The importance of a concept is the level to which it prevents conflict and damage and/or the extent to which it improves the quality of life.

Meta-positivity exists only slightly above equilibrium because if we move too far away from equilibrium, we will lose meaning.

A traumatic event can cause attachment and damage because it represents an impulsive conceptual force.

Truth has no meaning. Truth has meta-meaning. Meta-meaning is action in stasis. It is the sound of silence. It is the cycle of our perspective on life. Meta-meaning is meta-positivity.

The third way is like poetry. It is what emerges from the balance between the literal and the figurative.

The cluster physical/emotional/intellectual is a significant whole that combines the inner and the outer universes.

When two thought patterns collide with opposite velocities, there is conflict. When one or both thought patterns emerge distorted or non-functional, there is damage.

Two thought patterns with opposite velocities have opposite meanings.

Purely abstract thought patterns are never in conflict.

Heat has minimal abstraction and meaning. This is consistent with the fact that it is difficult to extract work from heat.

The more concrete a concept is, the greater is its potential to become a representation. Therefore, the more meaning a concept has, the greater is its potential to become a representation.

We derive theories from abstraction and experiments from meaning.

A concept with charge has meaning. A concept without charge is abstract.

The velocity of a code is its rate of decompression.

Pure abstraction is unchanging. Therefore, pure abstraction is timeless.

When imagination is inconsistent with reality, it is not informative. Therefore, it has no abstraction and cannot be decompressed into something more meaningful.

A lie is not informative. Consequently, a lie is not abstract, but has a negative meaning.

Meta-meaning emerges from the absence of meaning. Suicide and murder are misdirected attempts to find meta-meaning by destroying meaning.

Abstraction is real because, conceptually, it is mass.

The third way is a path. There are many paths.

When we focus on the abstract, we release negative energy.

When we focus on the concrete, we release positive energy.

When our focus is balanced, the net energy is zero.

When complexity is large, there is a greater probability of inconsistency. Inconsistency creates heat. Intelligence is the ability to tolerate heat. Therefore, intelligence is the ability to tolerate complexity.

Zero=epsilon is the code for meta-positivity. That is, from zero emerges energy.

Zero mental energy does not preclude mental activity and thus, it does not preclude meaning.

The balance between meaning and abstraction is the balance between positive kinetic energy and negative potential energy.

Communication is an effort to share meaning.

Abstraction is invisible. Meaning is visible.

We begin with an isolated concept and minimal meaning. We then seek meaning in opposite concepts. We acquire meaning and are attracted to like concepts. Eventually, our concepts become homogenous and once again we have an isolated concept. The cycle repeats.

A thought pattern with high abstraction and high meaning is like a large mass with a high velocity. A thought pattern with low abstraction and low meaning is like a small mass with a low velocity.

A physics book has high abstraction and high meaning. A children's book has low abstraction and low meaning.

A concept has meaning only with respect to other concepts.

In the first way, there is no motion. In the second way, there is no force. In the third way, there is no energy. The third way can exist without the second way and the second way can exist without the first way.

The ability to produce stasis requires physical control. That is the first way.

The ability to suppress desire requires emotional control.

That is the second way.

The ability produce organized thinking requires intellectual control. That is the third way.

A proper conceptual cluster is neutral. An improper conceptual cluster is charged.

An improper conceptual cluster has negative meaning.

Corrections are meaningful if they increase organization.

Corrections are meaningless if they decrease organization.

Psychological heat increases mental pressure. Therefore, the third way reduces mental pressure.

Observe a concept. If, over time, it does not change, then it is real.

Reality is empty.

We seek meaning in ideals, because we are not sure they are real.

Love is an ideal. God is an ideal. Being rich is an ideal. Being famous is an ideal.

Ideals are real because they affect reality.

If we spend a lot of time thinking about something, it becomes real because it affects our reality.

In the sense that meaning is the rate of change of concepts, energy is the rate of change of information.

Mass is information per unit length.

Meaning is energy.

A conceptual cluster is an ensemble of interactive concepts.

Rules limit behavior. Abstraction defies rules.

When there is friction between two people, there are problems. Friction creates heat.

Essentially, momentum is abstraction times meaning.

In the inner universe, momentum is conserved, unless there is an outside force. This is the law of abstraction.

Random thoughts have no net momentum, but they can create an isotropic pressure.

An isolated concept eventually has no size because it develops infinite abstraction.

It is peculiar that for a thought pattern, the most massive is the smallest and the largest is the fastest.

It is straightforward to interpret a message that has meaning. It is difficult to interpret a message that is abstract.

When we encounter a constraint, it acts as a force and changes our momentum.

Truth has no velocity because it does not change.

The first way is the path to truth. The second way is the path to happiness. The third way is the path to knowledge.

Meaning is the action of seeking meaning. When that ceases, there is only truth.

We begin with nothing and we end with nothing.

Change is followed by truth. Truth is followed by change.

It is not that existence precedes essence. It is that essence precedes existence.

We make over babies because they are full of meaning. They are not abstract.

Pure abstraction is not a constraint. An ideal is not a constraint because abstraction defies rules.

Constraints have structure because they have meaning.

Meaning is consistent with experience. We often seek meaning in the material.

Our fundamental action is to seek meaning.

Every whole is a part of every other whole. Therefore, no whole is completely isolated. Isolation is an approximation.

Life is meaning. Death is abstraction. We love life. We fear death. We love meaning. We fear abstraction.

Knowledge is the rate of change of abstraction into meaning. Therefore, knowledge is the rate of change of energy. The rate of change of energy is power.

Since meaning is experience, knowledge is the rate of change of experience. Therefore, knowledge is manifestation.

The third way seeks to transcend equilibrium as dialectic.

That is, thesis meets anti-thesis and produces synthesis.

The third way is stable in its simplicity. It is isolated in its complexity.

The primary code is the two-tuple: whole/part.

When a two-tuple generates a two-tuple, neutrality is preserved.

A code produces knowledge. Therefore, a code produces power.

An error is a negative consequence of free will.

Abstraction enhances free will.

The more one contemplates abstraction, the more susceptible one is to error.

Meaning corrects error.

The two-tuples mass/energy and abstraction/meaning are equivalent codes.

The fields of influence created by concepts control the flow of information in a network. If those fields are not properly aligned, the flow will encounter resistance. The properties of the network are determined by the flow. If resistance diverts or blocks the flow, those properties will change.

When a network is consistent at one level, it may be inconsistent at a higher level. Therefore, a fundamental restructuring of the network is required. The third way constitutes a fundamental restructuring.

The clarity of the third way is its meaning. The lack of clarity of the third way is its abstraction.

The third way combines the inner and outer universes.

The third way aims to supplant the code given by circumstance with a code given by reason.

The sustainability of a new code is a measure of its ability to interface with existing codes.

There is a difference between a habit and the truth. A habit is an attachment. A truth is a fact.

The meaning of a fact exists in its contrast to other facts. A fact, in and of itself, has no meaning.

Everything is code. When a code is in stasis, it is abstract.

When a code runs, it has meaning.

A code will remain the same unless acted on by an outside force.

A force is a product of a code.

An ensemble of codes is a larger code.

A code is hot due to internal resistance.

A code is cool due to internal conductivity.

Cool codes are desirable.

The third way aims to be a cool code.

The language of code is a conjunction of all disciplines.

The smallest functional code is a two-tuple. That is, the smallest functional code consists of two concepts.

Communication is the interaction of codes. Therefore, communication takes place between conceptual clusters.

A code is a system.

The two-tuple start/stop designates the two basic states of a code.

A functional code cannot consist of a single concept because if it did, it would have no meaning.

If an entity had only one attribute, it would not be code. The condition of being code is the reason mass has energy.

Codes vary according to their structure. A whole is a code and a part is a code, but not every part is a whole.

The exclusion principle keeps a code cool.

Adiabatic decompression and isothermal compression keeps a code cool.

Perturbations in abstraction can expand into extensive meaning. That is, abstraction contains a lot of rest-mass energy. Therefore, abstraction must be carefully manipulated.

Emptiness is code in stasis. Energy is code in action.

Psychologically, a code combines mass, energy, and information.

We can describe the relationship of the forces of nature to code:

The force created by a code that attracts or repels other code is primarily due to its charge. Charge is due to meaning. This force is electromagnetism. Gravity is due to the abstraction of a code. Abstraction is mass. The weak force causes the meaning of a code to decay. The strong force converts the interior meaning of a code into abstraction.

As a code produces knowledge, it extends its own meaning.

It is interesting to think of a psychological attribute as the color of a code. For example, honor, pride, jealousy, confidence, and integrity are all colors. In that sense, we can give a code a spectrum. This allows us to discuss the bandwidth of a code. A code with a narrow bandwidth could be an inanimate object, whereas a code with a broad bandwidth could be a human being.

White is the sum of all colors and black is the absence of color.

Consequently, a white code has maximal bandwidth and thus maximal diversity and a black code has minimal bandwidth and thus minimal diversity.

This analysis leads us to the conclusion that white is the color of abstraction and black is the color of meaning.

Just as white light expands into a dark room, abstraction expands into meaning.

It is a peculiar conclusion that, psychologically, white is empty and black is full, but physically, white is full and black is empty.

We note that our two-tuples commute. For example, mind/brain equals brain/mind. Therefore, white/black equals black/white.

We add the further stipulation that the color of emotional attributes is of longer wavelengths, near red, while the color of non-emotional attributes is of shorter wavelengths, near blue. Therefore, a code that is red-shifted becomes emotional while a code that blue-shifted becomes non-emotional.

There is a precedent in physics for using color to identify physical attributes for sub-atomic particles called quarks. In transpersonal psychology, color is the property of an aura. Of course, light has different colors.

A red code is emotional. This is consistent with heat.

The first way is a code with zero velocity. The second way is a code with zero force. The third way is a code with zero energy.

The first code is massive. The second code is blue. The third code is cool.

The unified code is massive, blue, and cool. This is a peculiar result of the projection of physics into psychology.

A code is software that processes information. Therefore, when we refer to everything as code, we are calling it software. This is consistent with the proposition of the physicist John Wheeler, when he said that the universe is "it from bit".

The mind is the final arbitrator and from that perspective, everything is code.

Every code consists of some combination of abstraction and meaning, just as in physics; every particle consists of some combination of mass and energy. By coupling mass and energy to abstraction and meaning, we merge reality into code.

The code we create is based on the pre-existing code we inherit from the universe.

This pre-existing code constitutes the constraints we have to contend with.

It is important to construct code with consistency and precision. Language must be carefully used.

This book extracts the meaning of a particular code.

Therefore, this book represents knowledge.

The meaning presented in this book answers significant questions.

Questions block flow. By answering questions, this book improves flow.

Flow implies meaning, that which we seek.

Causality is minimal when abstraction is maximal. That explains the subtle causality of this part of the book. In the third way, all fundamental concepts exist in a minimal space. Therefore, apparently discontinuous thought patterns are actually in close proximity.

At this point, there is a critical level of logical consistency.

REFLECTIONS

The third way is a method to improve the function and quality of life. It is a path to more meaning and an end to confusion. We want to understand why we are motivated to do certain things despite their negative consequences. The third way offers answers.

The universe places certain constraints on our behavior through genetics, physical laws, and societal laws. The inability to properly navigate these constraints limits our freedom and can cause pain and suffering. It is our conditioning and education that determines the actions we make to improve our lives. Unfortunately, this often falls short of the goal because the acquired knowledge is insufficient for the task. We tend to look for answers in science, religion, philosophy, and spirituality. Sometimes we are satisfied with this approach, but more often than not, this approach has limited results.

The worst-case scenario is that we succumb to the disorder in our lives and turn to addiction and violence. This creates a pathetic and often dangerous element within society.

There are three essential systems: the physical system, the emotional system, and the intellectual system. They are interactive and hierarchical in the sense that the physical system feeds the emotional system that in turn, feeds the intellectual system. We can think of them independently or we can think of them as a combination, such as within a human being.

In order to discuss these systems with the same language, we will project physics into psychology. We are using psychology in reference to the system of thoughts within the mind and or brain which we will designate mind/brain for short. Therefore, velocity can either refer to the velocity of a mass or the velocity of a thought pattern. Think of a thought pattern as being equivalent to a cluster of concepts or a single concept. So, just as we can think of a force as a quantity that accelerates either a mass or a charged particle, we can think of a force as a quantity that accelerates a concept. As a mass or a charged particle can have a force field that pushes or pulls on other masses or charged particles, a concept can have a force field that pushes or pulls on other concepts. In physics, energy is the ability to do work. With respect to the mind/brain, we will define energy as the rate of change of a concept.

For each system, there is a way to reach a higher state of being. Each way is a form of equilibrium or balance. The first way is equilibrium of velocity or zero velocity. The second way is equilibrium of force or zero force. The third way is equilibrium of energy or zero energy and it requires the absence of heat or the maintenance of high-grade energy. The first way suggests stasis. This could mean a lack of motion or a focus on a single concept. This way is consistent with meditation. It might correlate to martial arts. Alternatively, it might correlate to technological development capable of precise physical control. The second way suggests passive resistance or a lack of desire. This is consistent with the suppression of emotion. The third way suggests the balance of negative potential energy with positive kinetic energy and the absence of heat. This is consistent with organized thinking.

There is a phenomenon in quantum physics that creates energy within a vacuum based on the uncertainty principle. It is a way for energy to emerge from equilibrium. We propose that each way produces a still point and emerging from each still point is a small positive energy. We refer to this energy as meta-positivity because it extends beyond the balance of positive and negative. Meta-positivity is non-dual in the sense that it exists beyond dualism.

It is possible to acquire each still point by using the proper meditation. This combines all three ways.

The third way includes two basic stages. The first stage is a meditation called meta-duality that deconditions the mind/brain from improper concepts. Meta-duality is being open to extremes. The continued interaction of extremes eventually results in the more cooperative concepts becoming dominant. At this point there is a lot of mental energy due to isolated concepts. The second stage of the third way, referred to as meta-conditioning, is to combine concepts into complimentary clusters. This is done in a way that neutralizes the effective force fields. These clusters contain negative potential energy similar to gravitational energy. They balance with the positive kinetic energy of mental motion to create energy equilibrium. It is important to remove heat energy that is highly disorganized. Ordering our thinking processes and employing the proper neutral clusters accomplishes this.

A conceptual cluster represents compressed information. Examination and analysis of a cluster will release or decompress this information.

The primary neutral cluster is whole/part. Because parts are indefinitely extended through interaction and exchange, every whole is a part of every other whole. So a whole is a part, but a part is not necessarily a whole. This cluster implicitly contains all other significant clusters. We determine this by examining the cluster. For example, every whole consists of parts, but the identity of the whole does not exist in a single part. Therefore, the whole is empty. Alternatively, each part is indicative of the whole. Therefore, the whole is full. This generates the cluster emptiness/ fullness. This cluster, in turn generates other significant clusters and the process continues.

Everything is empty, including emptiness. Therefore, emptiness is also full. The continual emptying of emptiness creates an endless cycle of emptiness and fullness. With this pattern, the universe endlessly expands and contracts. If we divide the universe into the inner universe and the outer universe, then both the inner and outer components of the universe cycle through expansion and contraction. This produces an endless cycle of life and death for both universes until one or both universes exits time.

We propose the law of abstraction. That is, the product of the abstraction of a thought pattern and its velocity is a constant unless an outside force acts on the system. Define abstraction as the information per unit length, in which we are considering implicit information. Then we find that a conceptual cluster is highly abstract. Comparing this to physics, we find that the law of abstraction is equivalent to the law of conservation of momentum, if we identify abstraction as being equivalent to mass. Consequently, if we compress a thought pattern, it becomes highly abstract and thus, massive. An abstract thought pattern moves slowly. This is consistent with the time needed to examine it. When a thought pattern has minimal mass, it has maximal velocity, consistent with the law of abstraction. It is clear that the minimal mass contains more kinetic energy. Since a decompressed thought pattern contains more meaning, we can correlate kinetic energy to meaning. Therefore, we interpret mass as abstraction and kinetic energy as meaning. This creates the equivalent clusters, mass/energy and abstraction/meaning. Based on dualism, the contrast of compliments or opposites is necessary in order to maintain meaning. This suggests that an isolated concept develops minimal meaning and therefore, develops maximal abstraction. We can also define meaning as the motive force behind the flow of information. This is consistent with defining meaning as kinetic energy. In addition, we can identify meaning as proportional to charge since charge is an element of current. Abstraction is information per unit length. Information, in this sense is implicit information. For example, whole/part contains maximal implicit information.

The rate of change of abstraction into meaning is knowledge. We are naturally attracted to meaning and we are naturally repulsed by abstraction. Abstraction is theory and meaning is experiment.

Random events contain minimal abstraction and minimal meaning. Randomness or entropy is a counterpart of meaning that expands and contracts with it. It is desirable to keep entropy isolated from meaning.

This is consistent with the exclusion of heat from the inner universe prescribed by the third way.

Both the inner and outer universes cycle from abstraction to meaning as they expand and contract. This is consistent with the interpretation of maximal abstraction as a gravitational singularity.

There are a number of different reasons for our attractions and repulsions. When there is a deficit of meaning, we seek opposites. When there is a surplus of meaning, we seek compliments. Reality is empty and thus abstract. Consequently, we are unsatisfied with reality. We seek ideals because we believe ideals have meaning. However, ideals are real and the sustainable path to meaning is through knowledge.

There is a non-dual counterpart of meaning that is called meta-meaning. Meta-meaning exists as meaning expands and contracts in an equilibrium with abstraction. Meta-meaning is a correlate to meta-positivity, since both meta-meaning and meta-positivity represent a small positive energy.

Abstraction weakens causality, because it is akin to a gravitational anomaly. Therefore, if we are mentally invested with abstraction, our thoughts and actions have more freedom.

The primary goal of the third way is to maximize mental clarity and organization. When thoughts are disorganized because of contradictory concepts, the concepts can deform and attach to one another or disrupt and scatter. This can cause emotional problems, personality changes, and irrational behavior. Normally, we compartmentalize our concepts so that they do not interfere with one another, but that state is difficult to maintain as we respond to different situations in life. In addition, we lose the full potential of information if we are unable to integrate it.

In this book, we carefully define the significant laws of physics and psychological behavior in an efficient and unified way in order to optimize their field of influence. This creates more mental space.

What is important here is having a precise understanding of the major concepts so that the complex network of thought patterns produced by these concepts maintains a maximal consistency. This requires a very subtle use of language. As we process information, we absorb patterns that are integrated into our consciousness. Even if we do not immediately understand the information, it causally projects itself into our mental network and creates flux. In order for that flux to have maximal conductivity, the constituent concepts and their implications must remain coherent. This book is a meditation designed to imprint concepts even if they are only modestly understood. Most of the book has continuous organization. Some of the book is redundant. Some of the book is based on free association. All of these structures are intended to deliver the same message from different perspectives. Throughout the book, a conceptual consistency is maintained.

The third way is a method for producing mental equilibrium in terms of zero net energy. Negative mental energy designates internal exploration that moves from larger to smaller perspectives. This negative energy can exist as potential energy due to a conceptual cluster. Positive mental energy designates external exploration that moves from smaller to larger perspectives. This positive energy exists as kinetic energy. Heat energy instigates random motion and temperature increases. The third way excludes heat. In this sense, the third way is responsible for a cool mental state. This state has been compared to a superconducting state in physics that allows electrical current to flow without resistance. The comparison is isomorphic if electrical current is identified with a thought sequence containing a flux of concepts.

We have discussed how the forces of nature recognized by physics connect to the attributes of concepts. Gravity requires abstraction or mass. Electromagnetism requires meaning or charge. The weak force deteriorates meaning. The strong force converts meaning to abstraction. At the nexus between meaning and lack of meaning, electromagnetism merges with the weak force to become the electro-weak force. The three forces of nature can describe all of the phenomena of the physical universe. The significance of the isomorphism between the forces of nature and forces on concepts is that it combines the inner and outer universes and further prescribes that all psychological phenomena can be described by the forces due to abstraction and meaning. For example, we might imagine that the unconscious is isomorphic to dark matter, the undetectable mass the universe is largely comprised of. Consistently, we have already proposed that abstraction is invisible.

Meta-positivity manifests in a different form for each way. The first way manifests truth. The second way manifests happiness. The third way manifests knowledge. The first way requires stasis or a single, isolated concept. An isolated concept is empty and devoid of meaning. Reality is empty. Therefore, the first way yields the truth of reality. The second way requires zero force or lack of desire. This removes stress and therefore, it yields happiness. The third way requires zero energy, including zero heat. This creates mental clarity and therefore, it yields knowledge.

Anything that has an impact on reality is real. Therefore, ideals are real and thus, empty. Change, knowledge, and experience all have meaning. An isolated concept loses meaning. However, we need both abstraction and meaning in order to reach equilibrium.

Knowledge is power. Knowledge is the rate of change of abstraction into meaning. Power is the rate of change of energy. The conversion of abstraction into meaning is isomorphic to the conversion of mass into energy. Knowledge is like a nuclear reaction.

Isolation is an approximation. Nothing is ever completely isolated. This follows directly from whole/part and points to the infinite connectivity of the universe.

Our paradigm simplifies greatly when we define everything as code or software. The purpose of code is to process information. We can delegate this operation to the mind. Different codes process information in different ways. In the inner universe information is contained in a concept. From this perspective, every action, every object, every feeling, and every thought is code. Code creates force that attracts or repels other code. Code is hot or cool due to its level of organization. Code is abstract and has meaning. Code has mass and energy. Code has color due to its spectrum of attributes like, honor, integrity, jealousy, pride, or happiness. Red specifies emotional attributes and blue specifies non-emotional attributes.

The smallest code is a single concept. The smallest functioning code is a two-tuple like whole/part. We point out that these particular two-tuples commute so that whole/part equals part/whole.

The third way creates code that is cool. Of course, the third way is also a code. Codes cycle between being massive and small to being energetic and large. These physical attributes are isomorphic projections from the outer universe into the inner universe. The combined code of the first, second and third ways produces code that is massive, small, blue, and cool.

It is the intention of the third way to promote knowledge by conditioning the mind to function more efficiently. The approach is to sort out the elements that interfere with mental clarity and develop a science of the mind based on isomorphic constructs from physics. We determine mental forces that are isomorphic to the three fundamental forces of nature. Therefore, these forces form the basis of all mental phenomena. Attributes based on these forces, including those that are yet to be explored, are definitively accurate because of the scientific validity of the three forces of nature. The focus on code correlates to the new paradigm in physics that identifies the fundamental component of reality as information.

ABOUT THE AUTHOR

The author Louis Houston is currently a research scientist at the Louisiana Accelerator Center at the University of Louisiana at Lafayette and has been in academia for nineteen years. Prior to academia, the author was a research geophysicist for Exxon. He has three degrees, including a PhD in physics from Rice University in Houston, Texas. His work has been focused on imaging problems in seismic theory, but currently involves applied mathematics. The author has a diverse range of interests which include painting and music. In both of these areas, the author has worked professionally. He has a strong interest in quantum mechanics and information theory, but also has interests in philosophy, including Eastern philosophy. The author has always treasured the pursuit of knowledge and the support of family members and close friends. Communication is considered to be very important and is a primary motivation for writing. The author lives in Youngsville, Louisiana and commutes regularly to Lafayette, Louisiana to work and to visit his mother. He has two sisters and maintains a close relationship with both. Music is an important factor. When he is not listening to music, the author entertains himself on guitar. He has personally produced several CDs of original music.

www.ingramcontent.com/pod-product-compliance
Lightning Source LLC
LaVergne TN
LVHW042247070526
838201LV00089B/64